Unbroken Trust

Unbroken Trust

Jill Anderson

**SIMON &
SCHUSTER**

London · New York · Sydney · Toronto · New Delhi

A CBS COMPANY

First published in Great Britain by Simon & Schuster UK Ltd, 2012
A CBS COMPANY

1 3 5 7 9 10 8 6 4 2

Simon & Schuster UK Ltd
1st Floor
222 Gray's Inn Road
London WC1X 8HB

www.simonandschuster.co.uk

Simon & Schuster Australia, Sydney
Simon & Schuster India, New Delhi

A CIP catalogue record for this book
is available from the British Library.

ISBN: 978-1-84983-788-0

Typeset by M Rules
Printed and bound by CPI Group (UK) Ltd, Croydon, CR0 4YY

This memoir is dedicated to Paul Anderson

Contents

Part I   1
Part II   17
Part III   107
Epilogue   287

Acknowledgements   293
Dignity in Dying   295

PART I

My function is merely to draw matters to your attention in an effort to make your decision easier. I would like to make some observations on sympathy and prejudice. There is no room in any criminal case, whether it be this one or any other criminal case being tried in England or Wales – or anywhere else – for sympathy or prejudice.

The defendant has chosen not to give evidence. The defendant, of course, has the right to remain silent. You may think you would have been assisted by the defendant's account of the events and, in particular, three matters upon which she could have assisted you.

She might have been able to assist you with why she did not seek medical assistance when Paul Anderson told her that he had taken enough this time. Secondly, why did she say different things when she gave her witness statement on the one hand and when she was interviewed on the other? Then the third matter – what was so different about the 17th and 18th July 2003 when she did not summon medical assistance and those other occasions when she did?

From the Prosecution's closing speech

17 July 2003

The day hummed. The sky turned from indigo, turquoise, flamingo pink to blue, deep blue, and then lighter. I stirred from the blow-up bed that I now slept on in the lounge. He lay upstairs. I began my daily routine. I washed, ate some toast and took him a cup of tea. He had moaned throughout the night. I knew he did not want to, but he had been so quiet for so long. He could not look at me; I could not look at him. I could not hug him: it hurt too much. I could not sleep next to him, as my movements beside him increased the pain. I went to my wardrobe, took out some clothes and dressed quickly as there was so much to do. I knew he was watching me.

He asked, 'Why did you marry me?'

I replied, 'Because you're a wonderful man.'

He smiled. 'I haven't given you much of a life, have I?'

Many times before I had replied, 'You have given me everything.' But now, I did not reply. We had used the 'love' word over and over again to each other.

My movements were slower; my eyes felt as if they were tipped to the back of my head. He watched as I tidied the bedroom, picking up magazines, empty sweet wrappers strewn on the bedside cabinet and scattered on the floor, chocolates and biscuits.

Something was different on this day, as if the sun had risen in a different place or not risen at all. I shivered. I went into the office and started work. I was organizing interpreters for two conferences. The morning went quickly, making phone calls to the interpreters and clients, making sure everyone knew where they were going and what to expect. At about midday I went to the bedroom. As I entered he was watching a French horse race on the television screen. He switched it off quickly.

'Do you want some lunch?' I asked.

He shook his head. Then he asked me to fetch the disability form that we had kept for six months but had not filled out. 'We'll complete it,' he said.

I went to get it, then returned and sat on the side of the bed next to him. I dusted out the crumbs, from the night before. He propped himself up.

The form was tedious: sixty pages of questions on every possible level of disability a human being can have. I read out each question and as he responded I wrote down his answer in pencil. As I turned each page, he was scoring a high mark on every disability, apart from anything related to his mental health, which was intact. At about 2 p.m. the form was half-finished.

He said, 'I'm too exhausted to continue today. We'll do it again tomorrow.'

As I went out of the door, holding the form, I told him I would go to the Citizens Advice Bureau in Ripon, as I'd been told. The form was already out of date and the suggestion from the CAB was to fill this one out as a dummy and then they would check it and help me send off for another, up-to-date one. He nodded and slumped back against the pillows.

'Do you want any lunch?'

He shook his head.

Filling in forms always made me so sleepy, I asked him if he would mind if I took a nap.

He said, 'No, not at all, you rest.'

I slid away. We could both hear the humming of the day. It was hot, about 28 degrees, the 17th of July 2003. He must have made his decision. I had written all his pain down on the form in black and white. He could hardly lift his wasted arms. He knew the deterioration would spread to his legs soon.

I slept for an hour perhaps and then I returned to check on him. Everything was the same; he was just quieter than normal.

'Did you have a nice sleep?' he said.

'Yes, I feel better.'

There was something different about him, a distance.

'Would you mind if I take the rest of the day off?'

'No, not at all. You do what you need to do.' He smiled.

'I have to go out and get some food. I'll go to Pateley Bridge and have a walk and then go to the new Italian restaurant and get a cheese and tomato pizza to take away with me,' I said.

He looked small and pale; his teeth were gritted.

'Are you sure you don't want me to get you to hospital?' I said.

'No.'

He was adamant. I left.

I got halfway across the moors to Pateley Bridge and pulled over in a place where we had stopped many times before: a place where you could see for miles. On a clear day, York Minster was visible, and beyond, the giant cooling towers at the power station near Selby. Now I could not see at all; my head felt foggy, I was distracted with worry. By instinct, I returned home to Paul. I stopped by the back porch door, where I was growing some sweetpeas. They had opened for the first time that day. I picked them, filled a small glass vase with water and carried them to the bedroom. I had been telling him about their progress. I placed them on his bedside cabinet. He looked at me, but there was something faraway about him.

'Don't do anything silly,' I said.

'I won't,' he said.

'I have to go and get us some food, there's nothing in the fridge. I won't be long.'

'Before you go, can you bring me some whisky?'

I went downstairs and returned with a bottle I had bought recently. He did not drink much alcohol but I had got a special bottle of whisky, Marks & Spencer's own brand, in case he asked. I gave it to him, even though it was mid-afternoon and he never asked at this time. I did that and I don't know why. I did not pour it into a glass for him. He levered the bottle between his hands and elbow as he was taking a sip. Then I took it from him and made a space for it on his bedside cabinet amongst the boxes of medication and his white china cup with the picture of woodland creatures on it. He kept this cup by his bedside so he could drink water during the night. I had to go. I did not want to. I would do it quickly, as fast as possible. I would drive dangerously.

I wasn't gone long, maybe an hour. It was a twenty-minute drive to Ripon, twenty minutes around Safeway's supermarket, twenty minutes to return. I bought the pizza and southern fried chicken that I could save for tomorrow's meal, I thought, and a few other items: milk, bread, butter, fruit juice. I hurried back to the cottage, dumped the shopping bags in the kitchen and ran up the stairs. He was sitting on the edge of the bed, clutching the mattress, with his back to me.

'What's wrong? Has anything happened?' I said.

He turned ever so slightly. 'I'm sorry. I've taken enough this time.' Then he rolled back down. There was a note on top of him. I picked it up. It read: 'I'm sorry. I can't stand the pain anymore, I love you. Your Darling Bear Paul.'

The empty packets of pills he had taken were on his bedside cabinet. I could not look at them or touch them. I tried to move towards them but I could not. My heart was beating fast. I had the sense that everything was preordained, that nothing I did now, whatever action I took, would make any difference. He had been saying goodbye to me for months. I had to accept this. I had cajoled, reasoned and now I could do so no longer. I felt defeat and resignation. I hoped it was not enough; he would wake, but if not, then I had to allow him his independent choice. It was 6 p.m. The hot air was cooling. A rose pink light fell into the bedroom. I made sure he was comfortable, and he slept deeply. I tried once more to look at the pills but could not. I picked up the whisky bottle: it was almost full, he had taken only a few sips. I carried it down to the kitchen and put it back in the cabinet.

The evening and night went quickly or slowly, I really did not know. I watched the deep orange of the sunset. Everything glowed on this summer's night. I was awake all night. I sent emails to two interpreters about the conference. I cleaned the brass fire stand and the brush and the shovel. I returned to the bedroom often and stroked his face and wiped the sweat from his forehead. I lay next to him and talked to him, pretending he could hear. I picked lavender from the garden and placed it in his ambidextrous hands. He lay on his back and slumbered. I wrapped the duvet around him; his kidneys had given him so much pain. I had not seen him sleep like this for years. He was snoring loudly; I relished the sound, to hear him finally sleep.

The night was quiet. There were no owls, and the sheep in the field next to us were silent. At 2 a.m. he woke. He looked into my eyes and asked me to put his radio earpiece into his ear. He liked to listen to the world through shortwave radio at night. He fell back into a deep slumber; maybe he had not taken enough and would come back to me in the morning. I wished, I prayed. I said his mother's name, 'Isla, Isla, Isla.' He slept on, deeply, untroubled, at peace. I smelled the summer air drifting through the open bedroom windows: green grass, mown hay, musky blossoms. I had opened the windows so fresh air would surround him and fill his lungs.

We drifted through the night, it was short and it was long. When I lay next to him, intermittently, I listened to the thud, thud of his heartbeat. At about 5.30 a.m, I pulled back the duvet, and watched as first his feet, then his legs, and then slowly his whole body turned blue. It was a creeping deep purple blue. I had read an article about a local woman on a yachting trip who had drunk too much alcohol, gone blue and died, and I knew that this was the point of no return. I held his hand. It was limp and sweaty. His mobile phone was in the bedroom, but I was not going to make the call. I went down to the lounge and looked at the telephone on the windowsill next to the chair. There was a wonderful view of the countryside. The fields and trees, the hills and purple moors in the distance. I continued cleaning. The brass mantelpiece gleamed. I knew the authorities would be coming, nothing to stop them. I could hear his breathing. His snoring had stopped and he was taking short, sharp gasps. The end had to be soon; the release was coming.

I climbed the stairs once more and lay beside him. I watched the light change in the room. It grew to a pure, deep light. It would be another hot summer's day – the 18th of July 2003. He was still warm. I looked at his perfectly manicured hands and his long, jagged toenails, which he had refused to let me cut. I felt the first pangs of loss: his words and his laughter were gone. It was as though his soul was flying and I was lying next to an empty body that used to be Paul. His mind was switching off and I was allowing it. The cruelty of his wasting disease struck me. His breathing was shallow and slow now, each breath a gurgle.

At 9.30 a.m. he opened his eyes. I do not know why but I mentally recorded the time. He looked at me, then he spluttered, gasped and took his last breath, a deep sigh, and he was gone. He was lifeless. Nothing stirred outside. Hours before, I had heard the neighbours leave for work; they were hard workers and early risers. I had heard them walk past and call out for their dogs, but now I was alone on our lane that had no name.

I wanted a few more hours with him before I called the authorities. It was selfish but these moments were all I had left of him. I felt a strange euphoria; there was no physical pain in this place anymore.

18 July 2003

I called my family and some of our friends, the closest ones. The doctor arrived. He was wearing a crumpled navy suit and sandals with socks. He looked through me and went quickly up to the bedroom. He held Paul's wrist and checked for a pulse then listened to his chest with a stethoscope. He walked past me out of the bedroom; his face was ice cold and grim. I followed him downstairs.

'What happened?' he said.

'He was suffering too much,' I replied, and I told him everything as it had happened.

'I'm sorry,' he said. Then I watched as he sat down on the chair by the window and picked up the telephone on the windowsill. He dialled a number and said, 'I'm reporting a death at home.' His words seemed disjointed, out of sync, and came slowly at me one by one. He put down the receiver, stood up and looked at me. I followed him to the door, unsure of what to say. He had been kind to Paul and that was all I cared about. As he walked through the door and out of the cottage he looked back at me as if he was looking down a telescope. He was angry, I knew that.

I sat down and waited, as if in a dream. I felt empty, drained. The day was heating up and I felt sticky. I went back up to Paul and sat with him, but there was nothing.

About an hour later, a woman police officer arrived. I showed her up to the bedroom and I waited outside. I could hear her moving about the room. It was surreal: the uniform, the police car outside. It was the same officer who had come during the second suicide attempt, which was more of an accident. After a couple of minutes, she returned. She had black hair and what seemed like sensitive grey eyes. We sat down in the lounge: I was

on the settee and she sat in a chair opposite me, scrutinizing me.
She adopted a matter-of-fact stance and took a statement. I cried
for the first time as I talked. The officer scribbled. I said, 'He was
a bird with broken wings.' The officer looked up at me. 'I have
to make another phone call,' she said. She left the cottage and
stood outside.

I needed to see him again, so I went back up. He was so
motionless. I moved a pile of magazines and I picked up his
china cup. Then I went downstairs and washed it and placed it
among our other china cups in a cupboard. The police officer
came into the kitchen. I was standing at the sink gazing out of
the window. 'Would you like a cup of tea?' I asked.

It was not long before three more police cars were parked
outside the cottage. Police officers entered in what seemed like
a stampede. They wore plastic forensic suits and gloves. I stood
in the centre of them as they buzzed about examining our home.
A clutch of them went upstairs to the bedroom where he lay, and
a photographer took pictures of him and the room. A woman
police officer shadowed me; another officer came up and asked
me where the cup was.

'What cup?' I replied.

'The one by his bedside,' said the officer.

'I washed it up.'

A burly, thick-set officer, who seemed to tower over me,
introduced himself as a detective constable and said, 'I have to
ask you some nasty questions and take a statement. Do you feel
you can do that?'

I said, 'Yes.'

'Let's go outside,' he said. He led the way.

We sat at the table Paul had made for me. The garden was
picture perfect. I had worked hard to make it like that for us. I
told the police officer the truth and he wrote it down. I kept

looking at his large hands with stubby fingers, which were stained with nicotine. He asked questions in a measured tone, but I felt uneasy. Then he asked me to read the statement. I could not. He asked me to sign my name at the bottom of the page confirming that what I had said was the truth. I did.

When we went back inside the cottage, they were carrying Paul down the stairs in a body bag. I wanted to touch it but I could not. I followed them outside and watched at the gate as his body was loaded into an ambulance. The DC approached me and said, 'I live in a real cottage with real slate tiles.' I looked at him; his words meant nothing to me. I was numb. There was yellow tape surrounding the cottage. I watched as the procession of police cars and the van carrying Paul's body moved into the distance.

19 July 2003

I had to see him. I insisted and my mother drove. We went to Harrogate, twenty-five minutes through the countryside to reach the town's car-congested streets and sedate rows of Victorian semis and terraces, then another forty-five minutes through the town to reach Harrogate District Hospital. I considered, for some reason, that I had never seen the seedy end of town. We arrived at the hospital, now so familiar, and went to reception to ask for the morgue. We were told to wait. I felt there was something strange about the receptionist's expression. Another woman came and led us through the hospital corridors. I made small talk with her but she did not seem to know much about hospitals.

We entered a room where the woman said he lay in an adjoining room and that they had brought him out of the mortuary. While we went through, she stayed in the next room with the door ajar. For some reason I wanted to close that door and have privacy, but I did not. Some animal instinct made me want to get to him before all else. He lay on a narrow hospital bed and was covered with a sheet. I touched his stone-cold face and talked to him, tears rolling down my cheeks. My mother pulled me away. I had to go. Later, in the evidence against me, a statement turned up from the woman at the hospital morgue.

20 July 2003

I lay in our bed and hugged anything that smelled of him: the pillows, the sheets, his dressing gown, the neck brace he had been using to hold his head up. I did not want to get up. My mother and brother had come on the night of the 18th and we had eaten the tomato and cheese pizza and southern fried chicken. They had listened as I talked through tears. I wondered if I would ever stop crying. Now my mother was not here; she had returned to look after my stepfather, forty minutes' drive away. My brother had gone home to his family in Manchester. Friends had offered to stay but they all had families, or jobs, or both. Flowers, cards and emails kept on coming. I placed the cards on strings almost as if they were Christmas cards. I wrote a tribute to him and emailed it. The neighbours who lived opposite our house offered their sympathy and asked if they could do anything. I declined, preferring to hide my agony. I thought of these things as dawn arrived and I forced myself to get up. I looked in the bathroom mirror at my sore red eyes. I went downstairs and kept on making cup after cup of tea and then moved to the office where I shifted papers around the desk. I had to make business calls. I would have to tell the translators who were working for us. I heard the post thud through the letterbox in the porch and made the journey downstairs.

In the stack of mail there was a packet. I opened it immediately. Inside were gifts that he had chosen for me on the Internet nine days before. We had won a prize and he was excited and went through the process of clicking all the buttons and accepting it. The prize was two CDs. He had looked at me and asked, 'What would you like?' I had replied, 'You choose.'

And there was the packet on the 20th of July 2003. There was a CD of Spanish for beginners and another that was an encyclopaedia of family health. These were some of his last gifts. There would be other things I would find that he had left for me. When I needed to make a call on my mobile phone, which we had bought just a few months before, I found to my surprise that he had programmed in two of my best friends' telephone numbers. How had he done that? He must have used my address book and my mobile when I was asleep. How had he found the numbers or worked them out? My address book was a maze, virtually indecipherable and a monolith of cross-referenced numbers. Somehow, he had worked out which number belonged to which friend and put them in for me.

I held the Yellow Pages in my hands and started calling funeral services in the area. I could hardly talk; the words in my mouth were glue. I called three services and each voice was experienced and friendly, discreet and not too invasive. I found one funeral service I liked in Harrogate. They could cremate him in twelve days' time. I booked their services and then called everyone to let them know. Then I called the coroner's office in Ripon to see when his body would be released. The receptionist put me on hold, then a male voice answered and I felt instinctively unsettled.

30 July 2003

I was in the bedroom at about mid-morning when I heard a knock on the door. I looked out of the window. It was the detective constable who had interviewed me and another police officer with him. I went down and let them in. They followed me into the lounge and suggested that I sat down. I sank into one of the armchairs and looked up at them; they remained standing. I was shaking. DC Richardson cleared his throat then cautioned me on my right to silence. I was being arrested for assisted suicide and manslaughter. Shivering all the while, I asked them if they were going to put me in a cell. They said no. They asked me to report to Harrogate police station the following morning. I said, 'He was only forty-three years old. I have to live with this for the rest of my life.'

After they had gone, I called my mother and told her what had happened. She said she would get advice. I put down the telephone receiver and paced around the cottage; I did not know what to do. My mother called back. A family friend was a former coroner for West Yorkshire. He would see me that afternoon. My mother came and we drove over the moors to his home on the outskirts of Skipton. It was a comfortable house in a hamlet nestled into the side of a hill. It seemed to have many levels as we climbed a series of stairways to a room overlooking a dell. It appeared to be his snug and office. He sat to one side of his desk. There were shelves with books all around us. I had met him before at my mother's wedding to my stepfather.

He listened reverently as I wept and related the story. He said in all his years as a coroner he had heard of nothing like this. He added that he had a friend who was considered to be one of the best solicitors in the area. He called him. We waited until he came: he dropped everything at his office in Skipton and was with us in half an hour. He was a tall, dark man and I liked him. I felt some reassurance in the company of these men. They both listened to what I had to tell them. The solicitor told me not to worry and that he would see me at Harrogate police station in the morning.

31 July 2003

Another beautiful summer's day. Butterflies and seeds drifted in
the creamy air seeking nectar and earth. My mother drove me
through all shades of green to get to Harrogate. We reached the
police station. I was led to an immense reception desk from
behind which three male police officers surveyed me. One of
them asked me for my house keys and searched my bag and then
returned it to me. After some other formalities, I was taken into
a tiny beige-coloured room with no windows. I sat down at a desk
opposite DC Bosomworth and DC Richardson with my solicitor
sitting next to me. The solicitor's long, thin legs nearly touched
mine and the cuff of his expensive shirt brushed my arm. I could
hear the rumble of a distant air-conditioner. DC Bosomworth's
eyes were hawkish. I imagined him eating an enormous, greasy
breakfast, or a large quantity of doughnuts. My husband was in
a fridge at Harrogate District Hospital. He had been there for
thirteen days. I pulled at the scarf around my neck, undoing it
and retying it, twisting it. It was the scarf that I treasured; the
leopard print one. It had been a present from my mother-in-law.
DC Richardson was benign and somehow serene. I wondered if
he had eaten porridge for breakfast, or a grapefruit with no
sugar. My solicitor twitched next to me. I wondered if he suffered
from a nervous tic. DC Bosomworth informed me of my rights;
I was cautioned and reminded of why I sat facing them. He then
softened his voice. He asked me if he could call me 'Jill'. The
shadow of what might be a smile moved across his face and then
it was gone. I felt sweat dripping down my back. My polyester
blouse stuck to me underneath my jacket.

PART II

Police Interviews: Harrogate Police Station
Tape 1: 31 July 2003: 11.24–12.00

DC Bosomworth   You've been arrested, Jill, by myself. Is it all right to call you 'Jill' first?

Jill Anderson   Yes.

DC Bosomworth   OK, you've been arrested on suspicion of involuntary suicide, sorry involuntary manslaughter and aiding and abetting suicide. Again you're nodding but do you understand why you've been arrested?

JA   I understand why I've been arrested.

DC Bosomworth   I know it's sensitive and I know it's upsetting but it's in connection with the death of your husband, Paul Anderson.

JA   Yes.

DC Bosomworth   Can you tell me how long you've been married?

JA   Eight years. We got married on the 24th March 1995.

DC Bosomworth   And again, you don't have to answer this question, but was it a good relationship?

JA   It was wonderful.

DC Bosomworth   Happy times.

JA   Very happy.

DC Bosomworth   I believe Paul was ill.

JA	Yes.
DC Bosomworth	Was he ill when you met him?
JA	No, we were together for ten years and ten months in total.
DC Bosomworth	Right, yeah.
JA	Prior to getting married, that was two years.
DC Bosomworth	So you'd been going out for a couple of years before you were married?
JA	Yes.

September 1992

His face was small and oval. He had sensitive blue-green eyes. It was his sensitivity that drew me to him. A group of us were sitting in a bar called Henry's in Richmond-upon-Thames. It was on the riverbank, which everyone agreed was a great location. It was a large place with a central bar and was packed with people eating and drinking. My friend Annabelle had enticed me there. It was one of her favourite 'after work' bars, a good place to mingle. There were five of us round the table: Paul, Annabelle and me, and two of Paul's friends, John and Pervas from Iran. Annabelle introduced everyone to me. I was talking about whether Rabin would make a difference to the Palestinian-Israeli conflict. Nobody was listening to me. Except Paul. Paul was listening to me and looking at me.

We left together. Annabelle had wanted me to go with her, but my loyalty was divided: I went with him.

The night before, I had sat on my balcony in Putney and said to myself, 'I will never meet anyone to spend my life with.' I had been on dates but I had not had a relationship for many years. It was my birthday. I had cards and gifts and I worked all day but had no one to come home to and share it with. So that is how I am able to remember the exact date when I met him, the day after my birthday.

I had not wanted to go out – and now here I was walking by the river with him.

I had been working into the evening, as usual. I was working in a production office at Twickenham Film Studios. My title was Production Secretary for a TV drama called *The Good Guys*. The first director regularly regaled the production office crew with stories of when Jack Nicholson came to town and the watering holes he frequented. I had been contracted for nearly six months' work but we were winding down now. Seven people had been fired over the course of the production. I had survived and I was glad it was all coming to an end in three weeks' time. I was wearing brown, thick-rimmed glasses and my hair was greasy, yet Annabelle had put me here beside him.

'Come out, come out,' she had persisted.

'I want to go home,' I moaned.

'It was your birthday yesterday, we have to celebrate.'

I had shrugged. It looked like she would not give in.

'All right,' I had said, 'but I'm only staying out for a short time.'

She had grinned.

I looked at him now. He was smiling and so was I. We walked to my car in a small triangular car park just off the river. The water winked in the half-dusk of a warm September evening. The air was clear and we looked at the stars as we exchanged information about ourselves. He asked me if I would like to have coffee at his house. I replied that I would, but I could not stay long. I gave him a ride home. It was rare for me to do this for a stranger. But from that first encounter, I felt trust, hope and an instinct that he would not betray me. My instincts were right. He never did.

It did not take him long to win my heart. We popped in at his local corner shop in Twickenham and he chatted with the Asian owner as if they were friends. Then we went to the house that he shared with two others, a young man and a young woman. He made me a cup of coffee in a china cup. He put the cup on a china saucer and they did not match, but it was the simple act of putting the two together that endeared him to me. We went into his bedroom. It was painted peach. There was a bookcase that was ordered and methodical. A TV, bed, pictures, chairs and bureau filled the room. It was comfortable and tidy. An organized mind, I thought. The only item out of place was a pair of boxer shorts on the floor. Embarrassed, he put them away in a drawer. He picked up a book on a table by the side of his bed. It was a small, well-thumbed book, a Danish dictionary. He flicked through it and read words to me. He was a linguist and fluent in Danish. I sat on the side of the bed and listened to him speak. I liked him. I really liked him. His voice had a slight Scottish lilt. He was born in Dumfries and grew up in the nearby town of Annan.

As the minutes passed, we got closer and closer; then we kissed. The kisses became more passionate and then we were lying on his bed. I felt something bumpy under the covers and looked at him. 'What?' He looked embarrassed. I reached under the covers and pulled out a small, stuffed toy owl. It was orange and white and wore a tartan beret.

He blushed and smiled. 'Hooty,' he said.

I laughed and got up. He gave me a kiss on my cheek and I left.

He came to my home the next night and I cooked for him. We had another kiss. The week went fast. We talked every day on the telephone. He called me, or I called him. It was easy. He was easy to talk to. Then he came to my flat at the weekend and stayed.

In two weeks, we had made the decision that we wanted to be together. The obvious choice of space was my flat so he moved out of his house and I helped him to move in with me. I remember his housemates watching us pack up his belongings with surprise and amusement. This was a whirlwind romance. But we were happy and it felt effortless to live with him. It all seemed to fit together like a jigsaw puzzle. The only real adjustment I had to make was the way I made a cup of tea. I grew up in Sheffield and he was from Scotland: he showed me how he liked his tea and that was all we really needed to know about each other and our needs. He never read my CV and he was not concerned about my age, even though I was five years older. He loved me. Everything else, including the toilet seat which he always put down, just slotted into place. He had grown up on a council estate in a large family, and with many relatives and friends, so he was not selfish. If he ate a bar of chocolate, he always saved some pieces for me.

This case, whatever your view, is a tragedy. A tragedy for Paul Anderson, who took his own life; for his family who remembered him when he was well, and for Jill Anderson, who spent ... over ten years – wonderfully happy years – loving him.

From the Defence's closing speech

Tape 1: 31 July 2003: 11.24–12.00 continued

DC Bosomworth   So when did his illness start?

JA   He got a virus on the 21st of March 1995. Three days before we were married. Many people with his illness, Chronic Fatigue

Syndrome, have actually named the date and time they got a virus and thereafter never felt well again.

DC Bosomworth   What did this illness do to him? What were his symptoms?

JA   He started to feel unwell and initially we thought it was a flu bug and then a sinus problem. We didn't even connect it to the virus.

DC Bosomworth   When did you move to Pateley Bridge?

JA   It was in April 1995. We started a business and it was successful.

DC Bosomworth   So was it a type of business you could run from home?

JA   Yes.

DC Bosomworth   So basically you could do it anywhere in the country.

JA   Yes.

DC Bosomworth   Do you want to tell me what it was?

JA   It was a translation agency. We were getting a lot of work. It was fantastic and we were very happy, but then he started to become unwell. We saw many consultants and had a whole series of doctors' appointments and no one could give him a diagnosis. In the meantime, we decided to leave Pateley Bridge and find a country cottage because we thought this might help his health. We couldn't really think about buying a property because he had a lot of hospital appointments and doctors' appointments to attend and he was starting to spend time in bed. I remember that we saw a doctor who told him there was nothing wrong and to go home and take an aspirin, but he wouldn't accept that.

DC Bosomworth   How long ago was that, Jill?

JA   That was 1995 or thereabouts. He wasn't well; he was my husband. He had lost the colour in his cheeks and, to cut a long story short, our business was beginning to slide because we were going to hospital so much to find out what was wrong with him.

DC Bosomworth   Did you both go?

JA   He started off going on his own because he was well enough at that time.

DC Bosomworth   He would drive then?

JA   He would drive himself and I would stay at home trying to run the business and he'd go and see various consultants on his own. They could not find a solution to his health problems. This is a classic ME/Chronic Fatigue Syndrome medical history. Everyone with these particular diseases, because they are a group of diseases, are having exactly the same experience as we did, which is complete dismissal by the medical profession because there is no test or cure for these diseases yet. There is even conflict over the name of these diseases, which is why people use ME or Chronic Fatigue Syndrome. It is, however, an umbrella of diseases.

DC Bosomworth   When was he actually diagnosed with ME/Chronic Fatigue Syndrome?

JA   At some point he saw a consultant. I cannot

give you the year. I think it was '97 or '98. He became ill in '95.

DC Bosomworth Can we safely say prior to 2000 then?

JA Yes. I think it took about three years for a diagnosis that he was satisfied with, which was post-viral disability, and that's when we can trace it to the initial virus in 1995.

DC Bosomworth When he had his antibiotics for the flu-like symptoms?

JA Yes, he never felt well ever again after the virus. What I watched over a period of eight years was a long, slow decline of someone who prior to this was healthy. In London we played tennis three times a week. We did everything.

July 1993

We were lost in Surrey, somewhere between Guildford, Horsham and Dorking. We were sitting in our car on a country road. I had the map. Paul took it from my hands and turned it round. He traced our route with his finger until he had located exactly where we were. The road was narrow with hedges and trees on either side. We were in a breathing space between towns and villages, the ever-encroaching conurbations, out in the gentle Surrey countryside.

'Do you want to go to Haslemere or not?' he said.

'I don't know.' I looked at my watch. 'It's ten past four, it's a bit late. The shops will be closing.'

'We've been there before anyhow.'

'We can do antiques some other time.'

We were silent for a few moments.

'It's your fault we got lost,' he said. 'We could have been there.'

'Is not.'

'Is so.'

We looked around us. The heat was sticky; the car baking in the sun.

'You don't have to be so narky,' I said.

'Narky, yourself.'

I got out of the car. There was a slight breeze. It was a relief to be out of the city, where the concrete was smouldering. I looked over the hedge to be greeted by a wide view of green fields, nothing out of place, nothing misjudged. It was a patchwork of farmland; fields, hedges and trees marked out by centuries of grazing, ploughing and hoeing. We appeared to be on a ridge and the land rolled down before us. The sun was going west. I shielded my eyes.

'Get back in.'

'All right.' I got back into the car.

'Where do you want to go, then?'

'I don't know.'

We both stared at the map, absently. It was our day out after working all week.

'Let's go for a walk, find a footpath?' he suggested.

I nodded. Paul drove on as we scanned the roadsides for a footpath sign. After a few miles, we spotted one and pulled into a notch in the grassy kerb.

We walked into a narrow avenue of undergrowth, a green tunnel formed by trees and bushes. Beyond the scrub we could just make out high wooden fences running down both sides of the path. The shrubbery blocked out all sound. We walked on for what must have been miles. All at once there was a whirling in the air, a distant sound and a rush; hooves, many hooves, were pounding the ground towards us but we couldn't see the beasts. I grabbed Paul's hand. Suddenly the fence to the right of us, seemed to buckle as the force of many animals hit it. I got behind Paul.

'It's a stampede,' he said. 'Oh lovely.'

'You would say that,' I said. 'They're coming for us, they'll knock down the fence and trample us.'

'No they won't, they're just curious, probably heifers.'

'Or yearlings?' I said.

We could see nothing of them. We could hear snorting and shuffling beyond the fence, the scuffing of many hooves. I clung onto Paul's hand. We continued walking and as we went the herd beyond the scree and fence came with us.

'I don't like this,' I said.

'We won't come to any harm. They're probably bored, just want to protect their territory, see what's going on,' he said.

'Is this path ever going to open out?'

'I don't know.'

And then suddenly it did. The trees came to an end, and the high wooden fence gave way to wire mesh. Fields fell away before us down a great hill, with the South Downs in the distance – and to our right was a large herd of animals. Their bright doe-like hazel eyes stared back at us. There were about sixty of them. They were all looking at us with rapt attention. Their nostrils were flared, as if we might possibly be edible.

'Llamas,' we both said in unison.

'A llama farm,' he said.

'They're gorgeous.'

I moved to the fence. The llamas were all shades, from white to coffee, hazel, chestnut; some were white with splodges of brown and black on their heads and bodies. Their faces reminded me at once both of deer and koala bears. Their ears looked like bananas and they had short, squat bodies, long necks with pompom tails, and stubby legs revealing tiny hooves. I thought of them in South America, carrying packs.

'What are we doing with them in this country?' I asked.

'I don't know, probably being bred for their wool, maybe, or food,' he replied.

'I'll look in Asda next time I go,' I said. 'But I couldn't eat an animal like that, they're so cuddly.'

One of them nudged me through the fence and I tickled it between its ears. I stroked one or two of them. I remembered a friend who had two llamas and took them for walks on leads in the New Forest. I had never seen them before. I would ask her next time I called her. A few of them stood as close as they could to the fence and tried to reach us through the mesh. 'Food,' they seemed to say. When they had assessed we were no threat and had nothing to offer, they slowly moved away and started grazing. We continued walking.

Tape 1: 31 July 2003: 11.24–12.00 continued

JA   It was just completely normal. He did have arthritis, but it only flared up once a year. He suffered from the odd ailment just like everybody else. Yet I wouldn't say he was in excellent health. I would say he did have a compromised immune system to begin with and that's why he ended up disabled and bedridden over a period of eight years and fought a constant battle to get well again. We went bankrupt because of his health and we got ourselves into debt. We borrowed money and he just couldn't work.

DC Bosomworth	Right.
Solicitor	Sorry to interrupt. You said, 'we went bankrupt'. Is that right?
JA	Well, no. The bankruptcy was in his name, Paul Anderson.
DC Bosomworth	So how did Paul get into debt himself, then?
JA	We had borrowed money against the business succeeding.
DC Bosomworth	I don't understand the bankruptcy laws. It's not really my forte, but I would think that if Paul had gone bankrupt, he must have owed money personally.
JA	The business owed money.
DC Bosomworth	Right.
JA	I mean we'd borrowed from the banks, who had happily given us bank loans based on our previous figures, which were good, but his health started to decline. There was every indication the business would succeed. We had built up debt that we couldn't now repay so the only option was to go bankrupt. It was devastating. The only reason for the bankruptcy was because he had a disease.
DC Bosomworth	So it was almost a downing process from '95.
JA	From '95 I watched my husband decline and I started reading about his disease and I talked to around 400 people who either have ME/Chronic Fatigue Syndrome or are carers. I was involved with the support group in Harrogate. I just thought, I've got to find out. I went on the internet constantly.
DC Bosomworth	About that particular disease?

JA   About this disease. I wondered why the doc-
                    tors were reacting this way because every test
                    he had came back saying that there was noth-
                    ing wrong with him.
DC Bosomworth   And that in itself would be upsetting, I take it?
JA   It was devastating for both of us because we
                    both knew he was ill. He wasn't the person
                    that I had married.

March 2002

One of the nurses was coming from the doctors' practice to take blood. He had asked for this as he wanted to eliminate other causes of his illness. All I could think was, What else is there to eliminate? She arrived. She was tight-framed, dark-haired, practical and friendly. She looked at him with sympathy.

'How long have you been like this?' she said in a soothing voice.

'For nearly seven years now, and getting worse,' he replied.

She was holding his arm, looking for a vein to insert the needle.

'Not much of a life stuck in bed, is it?' she said.

'The doctors have been so dismissive,' I said.

'Yes,' she said, 'you're being treated like the cancer patients of the 1950s.'

We did not answer. She stuck a plaster on his arm and left. I could feel the cruelty of it all. I bit my lip and asked him again as I had before, 'Why can't you cure yourself? Your IQ is 192, for God's sake.'

He looked at the ceiling. 'What do you think I'm trying to do?'

I picked up some clothes that were drying on the radiator and started folding them into tight squares. He was motionless. Then he lifted a cup from his bedside cabinet and threw it through the air. It crashed onto the floor on the other side of the room. I went over and picked up the pieces.

'I would need a budget of millions, a laboratory and a team of scientists. It would take years of research to find a cure ...' His words trailed off.

I looked outside. March. It was windy and the yellow daffodils were crushing together as if for warmth.

I went to him. 'Stay alive, please. They will find what it is.'

He looked at me – there was fear in him. He had once told me his hearing was so acute that he could hear the grass growing. I could not imagine but only witness the pain he was in. Why did it have to be him? Why did it have to be us?

Tape 1: 31 July 2003: 11.24–12.00 continued

JA   He was losing his health and he was battling. He was still well enough to take a gentle stroll in the countryside, which he loved. We would do five miles, then it was four, then it was three, then it was two, then it was one and then it was 100 yards. In the end it was no yards at all, so that was that. Twenty-five per cent of people who get the disease end up very seriously disabled and my husband was one of them. I believe that this is because they initially have a compromised immune system. He did have a history of arthritis and those types of conditions, so this virus was

	able to enter his system and ruin his immune system.
DC Bosomworth	Have you been told that, or is it something you've worked out for yourself or . . . ?
JA	This is my own assessment. We saw various consultants at Harrogate District Hospital and I started going to every appointment with him because he needed support. I felt that this was the right thing to do because that's what the ME Association says.
DC Bosomworth	And was he asking the right questions, do you think?
JA	Yes, I thought so. The disease is recognized by the World Health Organization but it was not really recognized by the British medical profession until 2002, when the government issued a white paper informing doctors that they had to take ME/CFS seriously.
DC Bosomworth	It was a constant battle, by the sound of it.
JA	Physically, it was a constant battle for him.
DC Bosomworth	Do you have any medical qualifications yourself?
JA	No, I never wanted to know about this disease. We both said we would never wish this disease upon anyone. I have never seen that level of pain and it wasn't until I started reading about it that I knew he wasn't lying.
DC Bosomworth	Right, I'm with you, but you never doubted him?
JA	No. Obviously, there were moments because I'm human and we had our debates and arguments but we had a very healthy marriage.

One GP took me to one side and said he was
making it up in his head. I called the North
Yorkshire Health Authority and they said I
should get out of that surgery now. I went to
see a psychiatrist who works at the surgery
and told her exactly what he'd been saying.
Last year, the Surgeon General got the most
letters ever received about this particular
disease.

DC Bosomworth Can I ask you again about the last twelve
months?

JA   Yes, he had taken up fishing but couldn't cast
anymore.

DC Bosomworth Right, was that fly casting?

JA   Yes. He loved it. He could only go about
once every ten days; he'd just stagger up. I
drove him. He would throw up. I'd have to
open the car door for him.

June 2002

His rod hit the ground and he shouted, 'Blast.' His face was red
with fury. He bashed the rod again against the bank of the reservoir. 'Blast, blast.' Down it went. His hair was on end. He did
not notice the anglers scattered around the banks watching him.
He glanced at me; my eyes rolled and I looked away. I did not
want to look like I was with him. I wanted to distance myself. I
felt my face burn. I wished I were in a different country. He
bashed the rod again and, leaving it on the bank, he marched
away.

He had taken up fishing on his fortieth birthday. He spent
that birthday in bed, but when he could get up again, he went

fishing. His father had given him a beginner's rod as a present. The idea was that fishing would be good for his health on the premise that doctors recommend fishing to stroke victims. I went with him. It was a day out together. I read a book or day-dreamed.

Leighton Reservoir became our most frequent waterhole. A local man had a hut in the anglers' car park where he sold flies and reels. We became friends with him. In places the reservoir is 100 feet deep, dug out from the moor over a century ago. It is stocked with rainbow trout and brownies, some of them weighing about 20 pounds. Bleak, stark hills covered with short grasses rise to the horizon. A wood nudges the reservoir at the far end; beyond that is wild moorland. Some years ago, an enthusiastic hiker discovered a skeleton on those moors. When the forensic scientists examined the bones they found out that they belonged to a man who had lain there undisturbed since the 1950s. The cause of death was uncertain, but it was probably exposure. No wallet or identification documents were ever found, so his name and the reason why he was there remain a mystery.

Most of the anglers who frequented the reservoir were Geordies who travelled down for the day. We enjoyed the quiet, understated friendliness on those banks. Paul had read about the type of flies to use and the best weeks of the season from angling magazines. We had been to an angling shop in Ripon and become acquainted with the owner, Roland, and his colleagues. They fished locally and told us about Leighton and the other places to go. From then on they provided a change of company. The camaraderie of the anglers was something we both savoured. It was an escape for an afternoon, often turning into evening.

But now casting was starting to become impossible. He got

stabbing pain when he lifted his arms. He sat down beside me. We looked at the rod lying there. The anglers still watched in curiosity, waiting for another fit. I could not blame them. They hoped for some more action on this quiet June day. He knew I was embarrassed.

'Shall we go?' I suggested.

He looked once more at the water and the rod and stood up. He walked back to the rod and tried another cast; this time the line hit the water. The watching anglers returned to their own fishing. I heaved a sigh.

There were no fish that day. He could not get the line out far enough. Eventually we packed up our things. As we walked along the reservoir back to our car we picked up the usual conversations with the anglers we passed. It was always the same comfortable words about how many they had caught.

And then a tall Geordie lad approached us. He was swinging four trout in his hands. He said, 'I've got too many and I can only take two; you have none. Please.' He held out two of the trout and we accepted.

There weren't many fishing trips after that one. Instead, he ordered a clamp, feathers, twine and sparkly material from a catalogue and made flies in bed. He said he was confident he would return to the water. I replied, 'Yes. You will.' He enjoyed watching a programme about angling around the world on satellite television. He became particularly attached to the Australian fishermen and fascinated by the fish in those waters. He also liked a British programme that featured a fishing trip with two fishermen who always consumed a bottle or two of red wine.

They decided to get out of the rat race, to live in an isolated cottage away from people so that they could work from home in peace and

*tranquillity. They shared the work. They had a joint business; she
was the administrator and he was the translator.*

*Gradually, you may think that they were drawn into an unusual
world where everything centred around him and his illness. Not
going out. No friends round. No drinks at the pub. No going to the
club, the pictures or whatever it is. It was, in its way, you may
think, the strongest and most loyal of relationships. It was the wish
of Paul and Jill went along with it. They broke off all contact with
the family, and that, you may think, is the background to the
tragedy.*

From the Defence's closing speech

Tape 1: 31 July 2003: 11.24–12.00 continued

DC Bosomworth	So when did that stop? When was the last time he went fishing?
JA	When he couldn't cast anymore.
DC Bosomworth	Right. Do you know how long ago that was?
JA	About thirteen months. He started to get less movement in his upper back around that time and he was starting to get suicidal with the pain. I didn't blame him. He made his first suicide attempt and I got him quickly to Harrogate District Hospital. He was diagnosed with a frozen shoulder. Looking at his state of mind, most of the time he was positive and happy, but he'd just have these dips where the pain was so vicious that he'd feel suicidal.
DC Bosomworth	He'd had enough.

JA	Yes, that's what the doctors said to us. And then they'd save him and I would bring him home and the pain continued.
DC Bosomworth	How was he after that? Did he perk up a bit or not?
JA	No, because he was declining and I think his immune system was packing in. Now I've got time to think about it, because I was his carer for eight years. I was blinkered. I couldn't see how serious it was. He was still constantly finding new hobbies. He loved gardening. We did the gardening at the other cottage, Rose Cottage, and we loved it. We tended the vegetable garden together. He was well enough to do that but when we moved to Westowe Cottage he rarely ever went into the garden, which gave me an indication of how ill he was becoming.
DC Bosomworth	Indeed, he made you that table, didn't he?
JA	He made that table when we first moved in.
DC Bosomworth	Into Westowe Cottage?

October 1999

We had asked around and found a local timber yard. It was down a muddy track through pine woods not far from the cottage. We wished we had a four-by-four as our secondhand Vauxhall bumped along the track. We got out and looked around. We were standing in the yard of what must once have been a farmhouse with outbuildings; stacks of wood were everywhere, and the ground was strewn with wood chippings. We could hear the hum of electric saws from inside. There were about ten men

working there, stacking wood, driving fork-lifts or having a cigarette. The air was filled with the sensuous smell of newly cut
wood. A young man greeted us, big and sturdy with a bright red
nose, auburn hair and crinkly blue eyes. He smiled, revealing
crooked teeth. He was dressed, like all the others, in a combination of worn-out working clothes: ragged woollen sweater,
ripped-up trousers stuffed into wellington boots, and gloves cut
off at the fingers.

'We're making a table,' Paul said.

We had moved into a new cottage, called Westowe, and Paul
had overnight come back to me. His energy had returned, his
face was pink again and we had danced around the living room
on our first night. He had set up the computers in our new office,
made shelves for a downstairs storage room and was delighted
with the cream Aga in the kitchen. It was ancient and fired by
wood and coal. I had tested it and the whole cottage bubbled as
the Aga heated the water in the pipes. It had become so hot that
we had opened the windows to cool down again.

Paul handed the young man a sheet of paper with the
required number of planks and their exact measurements. He
had spent the previous evening working out the pieces of wood
he would need to make a table and benches ready for sitting out
on a summer's evening. There was a small paved area beyond
a large porch at the back door. In this porch, which doubled up
as a conservatory, we would grow tomatoes in the years to
come.

The young man took Paul's paper and disappeared into one
of the buildings. We were unsure of what to do, so we walked
around the yard and chatted to the various men working there.
Paul went over to one of the wood stacks and lifted a plank. An
insect scuttled out and disappeared under the next layer of
planks.

Later, after we had driven home with wood poking out of the car windows, I held the planks in the garage as Paul systematically measured them, marked different sections with a pencil, and used his electric drill to make the holes for the nails. The day turned to night as light on the horizon faded. I switched the light on in the garage. He hammered and drilled late into the night as I did what he told me and brought relays of drinks to him. Paul continued to work all the next day, and on the third day we carried a picnic table and two benches to the paved area and sat down in complete tranquillity. The table and benches were absolutely stable, every piece of wood exact and precise. We held hands across the table and smiled.

Tape 1: 31 July 2003: 11.24–12.00 continued

JA	His health picked up for a few days and it was quite extraordinary. It was obviously a relapse. I can't remember its proper medical name.
Solicitor	A remission.
JA	A remission. And we thought we were on the way, that he was turning a corner, but it didn't happen and he continued to decline.
DC Bosomworth	So can you go through the events which happened when he came back home?
JA	He was still in a lot of pain and they told him he had frozen shoulder. The good news was the consultant said it would ease off. As far as I'm aware, it's a very painful condition. He'd also developed a neck condition that gave him discomfort and he blamed himself for

that. I said, 'You can't blame yourself,' but he did. He said he came downstairs one night and just stretched his neck up and it clicked and that caused him more pain. He was diagonosed with osteoporosis. That's on his medical records. It was a combination of diseases at the end. He had previously been mobile enough to prevent this because he was moving around the house. He was conscious that he had to get some movement back into his muscles. He always longed for a healthy body.

DC Bosomworth	How long ago was that then?
JA	Eight months possibly.
DC Bosomworth	And what effect did that have?
JA	It was devastating for both of us. All we wanted was recovery because now he not only had a sore neck and a frozen shoulder, he had all of the other symptoms too. He'd suffered Irritable Bowel Syndrome, which eased off, then he had frozen shoulder, but in the meantime he was still getting pain in other areas of his body and these pains stayed throughout his illness.
DC Bosomworth	So what physical effect did the frozen shoulder have on him? What could he do at that time?
JA	He just started doing less and less. He had to develop other interests: reading books, magazines, watching TV.
DC Bosomworth	So he was moving around the house at this time?

JA   Yes.
DC Bosomworth   I'm aware that he had a further suicide
                     attempt this year.
JA   Yes, he declined greatly in this past year.
                     Every summer he'd taken an active interest in
                     birds even though he was confined to bed. He
                     read books and shared what he had read with
                     me. I learned all about the birds, their names
                     and habitats, but this summer, for the first
                     time ever, he had very little interest in them.

April 2003

I noticed him listening to something and he told me what he
could hear. There was a squawking sound coming from below
the bedroom window. It would rise to a high pitch and then
descend again. He said it was the sound of chicks as they waited
for their parents to bring them food. He struggled to sit up and
we looked out of the window, scanning the area below. It was
not long before we spotted an adult blue tit in flight and heard
chirping as it alighted with food. A nest must be lodged in a
crevice of the cottage wall. He sent me out into the yard. Guided
by the chicks' chattering, I located the nest in the wall. I ran back
upstairs and told him what I had seen: four or five blue tit chicks,
soft balls of fluffy down with tiny beaks and perfect talons.

I waited what seemed like an age for him to lift himself out
of the bed. He swung out slowly, feet first; he had an action, a
sort of a flip. His feet were bird's talons as they curled around
the bed frame and gave him leverage. He could only use his arms
as levers, from the elbow to the fingers. His shoulders were locking, making movement in his upper torso almost impossible.

In 1999 he had planned to put a camera in a bird box. He had attached the box to a tree within view of our bedroom window. He was going to trail the cables to the TV and then we could watch the whole process of nesting, brooding, hatching, birth, growth and flight. He had never managed to finish the job, but we had fantasized about this experience as we watched wildlife documentaries.

Now I did not look at him. His face was white-grey. We went downstairs. I went quickly; he followed. I waited, shifting about, at the bottom of the stairs. He brushed past me.

We went outside. I walked quickly to the nest and waited for him. He shuffled behind me and when he reached the nest he said, 'Come on then, come on then. Rise and shine.' The chicks immediately responded. They chatted and jostled for our attention. There were two older, fatter ones at the front and three younger, skinnier ones at the back.

We went back inside. The visit to the chicks had seemed to take a long time. I wanted to be patient. He snorted as he walked past, but not so much a snort as a sigh or almost a sneer. He walked into the lounge, crumbled into the chair by the window and looked out into the yard. I followed. The action of sitting was agony for him.

I couldn't think of anything to say so I said, 'I've sewn poppies for you in the garden this year. They'll be up soon.'

'Thanks,' he said. He continued to stare blankly out of the window and, without looking at me, said, 'I'm fucked.'

I got up and went to him. I knelt down and put my hands around one of his skinny ankles, then I let go. He got up and, as he moved away, he touched my hair.

Next the suicide note . . . the note that was found at the house. It is nothing to do with this attempt, but an earlier one.

From the Defence's closing speech

To my darling Jill,
I love you more than I could ever say.
I'm so sorry. I just can't stand the pain anymore.
Thank you for everything you have done for me.
Please try to have the best life you can.
I love you forever.
Your loving Paul

Paul's suicide note from his first suicide attempt,
using mouse poison

Tape 1: 31 July 2003: 11.24–12.00 continued

DC Bosomworth   Now we've been in here for thirty minutes, I'm just going to cover the last suicide attempt, not the one where he died, but the suicide attempt before and it's going to be upsetting for you.

JA   I started sleeping downstairs because he was in so much pain and I heard him staggering around upstairs. No, I'm sorry that's wrong.

DC Bosomworth   Take your time, Jill, it's all right.

JA   We had a wonderful relationship. I was still sleeping upstairs. I remember that second suicide attempt because what struck me was that it was a completely normal evening. We'd had our conversation. We liked watching the movies together, all of the normal things couples do and a nice goodnight kiss. I woke up at about 3 a.m. or 4 a.m. and he

was staggering around the bedroom, walking into wardrobes. I panicked and said,
'What have you done?' but he couldn't talk
to me. He was completely in a daze so I
called the ambulance immediately and got
him rushed to hospital. They took all the
medication that was in the bedside cabinet
and hooked him up to lots of machines.
They then did lots of blood tests and discovered he'd taken too much Zopiclone
among other pills.

DC Bosomworth Was that paracetamol?

JA   Paul didn't know and neither did I, whether
he'd taken paracetamol that night, because he
was in so much pain. They kept him in hospital as a precaution but he hadn't taken
enough to cause himself harm.

DC Bosomworth Did he leave a note at that time?

JA   No, I don't think so, but we were now
entering a period where there were other
suicide attempts and I didn't call an ambulance. I just saved him by persuading him to
live. When we got to Harrogate District
Hospital it was the same doctor that had
attended to him on the night of the suicide
and they put him on life support again and
he just slept it off. I went home briefly and
came back to collect him later on. He was in
the bed waiting for me and he just said, 'I'm
so sorry.' And I said, 'I know you're in pain,
don't worry.' Then I brought him home
again.

February 2003

He needed to go to the bathroom. He slowly edged his legs out
of bed. Carefully, he was able to swing out. His feet touched the
dark green, acrylic carpet with its pink flowers. He found a pair
of slippers. He had owned several pairs over the last eight years.
These slippers were navy blue with a fleece lining and, even
though they were only six months old, they looked much more
worn, much older.

He slept on the left side of the bed, away from the door to the
room. The other side was my side. On his side was a window,
smaller than another one opposite him. This window looked out
onto the landlord's fields. The land beyond the lane fell away. It
felt as if Westowe Cottage was on level ground, but here the
land also sloped downwards. The fields were surrounded by
rolling hills and in the far distance were the North Yorkshire
Moors. When the sky was clear, it was possible to see the White
Horse, etched into the steep side of Sutton Bank. It had been the
brainchild of a local schoolmaster in the 1850s and at his com-
mand his pupils had marked out the horse and then filled it with
white pebbles. The closest field Paul could see out of the window
was a 3-acre oblong, with the cottage at its uppermost point. The
section of the field in which the cottage lay was now fenced off.
The cottage had a garage at the back which was reached by pass-
ing through a white gate and crossing over a gravelled yard. On
the left-hand side of the cottage there was a small garden with
a giant oak tree at its centre. It was a shaded, peaceful garden
surrounded by fields, with the only other house visible belonging to our neighbours, a childless couple who were private but
not unfriendly. They lived in a big old farmhouse positioned
diagonally to the lane, so they had seclusion. They ran a family
animal feed business and were out for most of the day.

Paul put on his slippers and went to the bathroom, where he washed and shaved. He did not want to ask for help. He combed his hair by bending down. He was having difficulty lifting his arms up to his head so he was getting used to inventing new ways of manoeuvring around the cottage.

The cottage had been a farm shed and its conversion was slapdash. It was a small whitewashed building with a red tiled roof and a white picket gate. The internal walls were painted magnolia and no surface was even or flat, all the stonework lopsided. The bedroom was above the lounge and both were big rooms. The bedroom floor sloped and sagged in the middle, but the room was warm. In one corner there was an old chest of drawers. Placed on top was a white fluffy teddy bear and Hooty, the toy owl.

The window at the end of the bed looked out onto a large, old chestnut tree. He knew the tree intimately; each branch, each season. Now it was bare. In the autumn, the children from the architect's mansion nearby, would sneak up to it and knock its branches for conkers. He had heard their raucous laughter as they collected their bounty. It reminded him of his childhood adventures; the excitement of returning home carrying secret treasures, a bag full of conkers to show his father and mother. The tree stood on the boundary of a field belonging to the neighbours' property on the narrow lane that ran between us. The field sloped upwards and was populated by our neighbours' ducks, geese and hens, which spent most of their time squabbling and looking for food. It was only the tree, not the lane, that he could see from his bed. At night, he could glimpse the shadow of the owls when they chose the chestnut tree in which to watch and wait, hooting. He liked owls: barn owls, little owls, tawny owls. We were mostly visited by tawny owls in the chestnut tree.

One Sunday he was bored with being in bed. He insisted on going out, the determination etched on his face. He allowed me to dress him. I slipped a shirt over his head and buttoned it, adding a chunky woollen sweater and jeans. I put his outdoor jacket on top. His bones were cracking and creaking as he lifted each arm to accept the sleeves. He looked at me.

'I'm clicking and a-clacking,' he said.

His outdoor Gore-Tex jacket was bright green with a purple collar. It looked Scandinavian. He could not lace up his brown leather walking boots. He had polished them when he first bought them, but now they were caked in mud. He let me do the laces. I felt guilty: I should have cleaned them for him, but there were so many other priorities. Then I put on my own boots, but he was impatient.

'Chop, chop,' he said.

'Almost ready,' I said.

'Why is spontaneity so difficult for you?'

'Because I've got a million other things to do, all right? My brain is jammed.'

I fetched the car, a silver Ford Fiesta, out of the garage. The reverse gear crunched because I had yanked it too hard. He walked to the garage as I reversed out. I waited for him to get in. He looked like a little old man.

'I'm a shadow of my former self,' he said.

He was irritated and difficult. He was going to lose it. I knew that. He had found something to pick a fight about and said he wasn't going after all. He got out of the car, slammed the door and stood looking out into the fields. There were a few scraggy crows in flight. More birds were perched on the surrounding fences, looking at us. One of them had a half-eaten worm hanging from its beak. The cows grazing in the fields ignored us. He pursed his lips and clambered back into the car. I fiddled in the glove compartment to keep my anger in check.

'Come on, let's not waste the day,' I said. 'It was your idea.'

'I know,' he replied.

We started the journey, turning right into the lane. He was slumped in the front passenger seat. It was a familiar route over Pateley Moor. We knew this moorland road in detail, as we had driven along it countless times. It was about 8 miles to Pateley Bridge up a long stretch of the lane. The route wound around fields and pine woods. Farmhouses punctuated the landscape. The lane was edged by slate-grey stone walls, slabs of stone that had lain in a wall for centuries. There were dry stone wall building competitions at least once a year in the area. We drove past a pub called the Drovers Inn. I had been in it once. When we were past the pub, we drove over a cattle grid and onto the moors. The landscape was a vivid purple in August when the heather flowered. Now it was green and murky-grey with soggy dark brown bracken lacing through the rough, short moorland grass. Ragged sheep grazed on it. They looked abandoned and their coats sometimes hung off them as if they had walked through barbed-wire fences and their fleeces had been mauled. They roamed free on the moor like gypsies or nomads, used to living rough in the bleakest weather.

We had spent so many hours exploring this region. The bird population was mostly grouse, lapwings, curlews, partridge and soaring kestrels, fleeting sparrowhawks and snipe. In the past, he had watched eagerly for any sighting of the local wildlife – birds, stoats and weasels. He would make up stories about them; give them names, occupations and personalities. He had lost interest now and gripped the dashboard with one hand and his stomach with the other. We drove on in silence.

It was wild and free. He knew I wanted to shout, 'Heathcliff!'

when we crossed Pateley Moor because I usually did. If I said it again I knew he would shake his head. We were not so far from Haworth, about 30 miles to the southwest. We had been in the area for eight years but still had not visited Haworth. He would have liked to have gone. I felt him looking at my face and I knew he was worried about me and the stress his illness was causing me. The regret between us was palpable.

We arrived. It was the open moor and the open road. Here at least was one of the quiet limits of the world. There was virtually no traffic and few people. Sometimes, if we travelled to Dallowgill Moor and took another winding road, it was possible not to see anyone at all and it felt as if no one else existed. Dallowgill Moor had one claim to fame: Bing Crosby had shot grouse on it. It had concrete hides strewn over it ready for the Glorious Twelfth, when the guns would ring out again. Nearby, a monument stood on the spot where the last wolf in the north of England had been killed around 1850 or so.

As we reached higher ground, the air became colder and icier. The moor looked tired of winter. It seemed to be flagging from the storms, gales, biting frosts and snow. It was ravaged and sore. I felt the moors were moody, like me. Bits and pieces of spent fern tumbled around on the road in front of us. The sky was washed-out grey-blue with a hint of yellow, and thin wispy clouds raced above. He hardly noticed. I was aware he was hanging onto himself, gripping and slouched. He was focussed on just getting there. I drove slowly. He would have finished the route in half the time if he were driving. I could not remember the last time he had driven. At least, his barking commands were no more, which was a mild compensation. He let me drive without comment. He gripped the dashboard harder.

We crossed over the final cattle grid, which took us off the moor and onto the road that stretched to Pateley Bridge. The ground was still high and we were among a crisscross mesh of stone walls and fields with no trees. There was the odd hawthorn bush bent by a gale. We passed a few grouse and partridge perched on the stone walls staring back at us morosely. Their feathers were fluffed up to keep out the chill wind that whipped across the open land. Their necks and faces were bent into their breasts with only their beaks protruding; but the sky and the landscape stretched into infinity and the place had a sense of forever. The roads had been pathways for monks in earlier centuries, selling their wares between Fountains Abbey, Bolton Abbey and Jervaulx Abbey. Castle Bolton, where Mary Queen of Scots had been imprisoned, was not far away.

We reached the top of the hill and now Pateley Bridge lay stretched out before us. It is a small Yorkshire market town, carved into the valley, with a reputation for wool and tin mining. Its houses are constructed in grey Yorkshire stone. We always paused at this point to survey the town below and its latticework of streets. Smoke rose from some of the chimneys. It was easy to spot the former workhouse, a large, obtrusive building of three storeys sitting at the top of one of the streets. How many stories would a building like that hold? He was not looking anymore. He lay back in the car seat with his eyes closed. I peeked at him. We were silent.

We started the descent, negotiating the steep, sharply bending road that led into the High Street. Tourism had taken over and the street was a medley of shops providing entertainment. There were several antique shops, a pet shop, a shop that only sold sweets and claimed to be the oldest sweetie shop in England, two butchers stating that they had the best meat in town, a grocery store run by a team of grumpy sisters, a variety of tea shops and eating places. The best place to eat was a 'greasy spoon', as no one bothered you and you could sit there lost in your own thoughts. There was a pub, The Crown. He had played snooker there when we first moved to Pateley Bridge in 1995. On the first Christmas we spent in Pateley, we bought presents for our families at the art gallery on the High Street. The shops were uniform in appearance, grey stone with white bay windows, green or red awnings, and flower baskets adorning most of them. There was a hairdresser, an electrical appliance shop, a bank, a building society, a posh upholstery shop and the new addition of an Indian restaurant. At the bottom of the street there was a Co-op and newsagent's. The people were friendly in these shops. Beyond the shops was the river that sliced through the town. It was a small river, but had a tendency to overflow in the winter and flood the bottom of the High Street. Once or twice it had been impossible to cross over the bridge that spanned the river. The town petered out beyond this point. Over the bridge there was a showground used for the Pateley agricultural show in September and as a caravan site over bank holidays. There was a park with a children's play area, war memorial and bandstand. The park led to a large permanent caravan site screened from the town by trees. The High Street finally ended with a few specialty shops and a petrol station, a garage and a rival pub, The Royal Oak.

We parked in the visitors' car park at the bottom of the hill before the bridge, by the café that hugged the riverbank. He said nothing. He sank back in the seat as I climbed out and bought a parking ticket. He waited as I went around to the passenger side of the car and opened the door for him to get out. He slowly dragged his body from the car, gripping me as he pulled himself up. I wanted to peel him off. We were tense. I saw the hairdresser locking up her shop and fading into the distance.

He took my arm and leaned on me as we started to walk back up the High Street. We looked into the shop windows as we had done many times before. Each step was hesitant and shaky but I guided him. We went into one of the antique shops near the top of the hill. It was difficult to remember how enthusiastic and filled with hope for the future we had been when we first set eyes on this street so long ago.

His spirits lifted. I watched him take pleasure in the furniture, the wood and all the old objects. If he could, he would fill our home with such treasures. He examined the display: brasses, pictures, books, chairs, tables, cabinets of all shapes and sizes, bowls, china, ornaments, stuffed animals in glass cases, fascinating pieces like surgeons' scissors from the eighteenth century, and Tiffany lamps, ancient linen, lace and silk scarves. There were glass cases of sparkling jewellery and we imagined the histories of the necklaces, earrings, gold rings and brooches that people had worn in another time. The shop was an Aladdin's cave of curios and *brocante*.

He walked over to an ornate desk, made from cedar or rosewood. It was beautifully crafted, intricately carved. He ran his hands over it and turned the key, releasing the flat top that made it into a writing desk. Between us, we pulled out the drawers, each gliding out smoothly with its tiny key sitting in a delicate gold lock. We examined all of the compartments and visualized the ink, the crisp writing paper, the letters, the cheque book, bills, quills, glue, elastic bands, paper clips and feathers. We mused over when it was owned and used. The shop assistant was a stout woman with a friendly grin. We asked her the price.

'Three hundred and forty pounds,' she replied.

Then he turned to me and said, 'Would you like me to buy it for you when I'm well?'

I smiled.

We left the shop and he could walk no farther up the hill. We went back down again. He was wobbly and stumbling. He used me to prop him up. He did not want to see anyone that we knew. He did not want to stand in the cold on the street and have to make small talk. He was not the man I had married. I wanted that one back. He wanted that one back. The one that was active, eager and alive, not this body. He was irritated and snappy. We reached the car and he had to let me help him in. He looked up at me from the passenger seat; despair belonged to him.

The journey home was quiet. We said nothing to each other as there was nothing to say. Only the hum of the car engine could be heard as it went back over the cold, silent moors, now edged with darker skies as the light dimmed. He was exhausted. I looked at him slumped in his seat as the disease took its toll. It was a short trip. He had only been out for about an hour and a half, but it was as if he had climbed several hills and walked many miles.

We pulled into the yard at the cottage and he had to wait for me to lift him out of the car. Then he had to use me as a walking stick to the front door. He climbed the stairs back up to the 'prison' and managed to undress himself. It was a last surge of energy before he flopped back into bed. I went through my usual routine, putting the car away, opening the coal bunker and bashing the coal until the bucket was full. Then I prepared the fire downstairs, something he had shown me how to do, as he had grown up with an open fire.

I eventually brought him his dinner and we snuggled down for the evening.

Tape 2: 31 July 2003: 12.26–13.07

DC Bosomworth Just at the end of the last interview, Jill, you mentioned that there had been other suicide attempts.

JA	Yes.
DC Bosomworth	Whereby you hadn't contacted the emergency services and no one knew about them.
JA	That's right.
DC Bosomworth	Would you mind telling me about those?
JA	Yes.
DC Bosomworth	Was that 'yes you would mind' or 'yes you will tell me'?
JA	I'll tell you.
DC Bosomworth	Thanks.
JA	My husband suggested to the medical profession that his disease was related to Gulf War Syndrome and both diseases have a very high suicide rate, which have been well documented. Now he's not with me, I've realized that he was in quite considerable physical decline. He was taking a lot of medication and in terrible pain. He had tried anti-inflammatories and steroid injections. I looked on the Internet and the only other treatment was using a laser. We were waiting for an appointment to see another consultant when he died. Prior to that, the last consultant who saw him told him that his cartilage was welded together so, as you can imagine, this was completely devastating news after an eight-year battle with his health where he'd had no improvement. His health was in a long, slow decline and he still had terrible pains all over his body. He still had frozen shoulders, his arms were starting to lock and his movement was becoming more and more

reduced. He was doing less and less because it was very painful, and he had even stopped combing his hair. I suppose that's when he started contemplating suicide on a more regular basis and I don't blame him. I don't see it as suicide but as escape from pain. On one attempt, which was unreported, he went off to the car and managed to chop up the hosepipe in the garage and put it into the exhaust.

DC Bosomworth   How long ago was that?

JA   I think it was about eight weeks ago. In the end, I managed to persuade him to just keep going and the conversation was always, 'They might come up with a cure or gene therapy. Just stay.' We were waiting for scans and he was going to ask a consultant at the Friarage Hospital for an MRI scan for his shoulders to see what type of damage had occurred and we looked on the Internet. We thought it might be a rotation cuff tear. I could not blame him for wanting to die, he was terminally ill.

We invite you to conclude that Paul Anderson chose to end his own life. You may be absolutely satisfied that Jill Anderson did nothing to encourage him in that. You only have to look at the earlier suicide attempts; getting the '999' call made and the ambulance to attend, or pulling the hosepipe out from the exhaust in the car.

It was his decision to end his own life with dignity, not in a sterile hospital ward after more and more years of pain.

From the Defence's closing speech

June 2003

Paul was angry. He couldn't help it. He struggled out of bed, dressed himself and went downstairs. He grabbed his keys from the set of brass hooks tucked on the wall between the lounge and the porch. The hooks were on a plate that featured two ducks and a duckling walking along. He had nailed it to the wall when we first moved into Westowe Cottage. All his limbs were failing. He knew I was watching him from the lounge window. He did not look. It was early summer and the air was sweet but he hardly noticed. I closed my eyes.

I waited, maybe five or ten minutes, then I followed. Paul had entered the garage. It was spacious with a solid concrete floor. He took down a green hosepipe that hung on a nail in one corner. He found a knife on the workbench that extended along the right-hand side of the garage and sliced off enough hosepipe. He found a rag, then attached the piece of pipe to the exhaust with the rag around it. He struggled into the car and threaded the hose through the driver's window, closed the window and turned on the engine.

He leaned back and closed his eyes.

The door opened. It was me. I pulled out the pipe. He ignored me, got out of the car, replaced the pipe in the exhaust and got back in. I waited and then pulled out the hosepipe. He got out and yelled:

'I want to die.'

'You can't.'

He listened as I gave him all the reasons to stay alive, ending with: 'The business will be a success, we'll make money. You'll get well.'

He screamed back, 'I hate you.' His face flamed red. For the first time in our relationship he slapped my face. I reeled with the contact. We glared at each other. He watched me as my face registered shock. But it was only a tap. I stormed out of the garage. I imagined him putting the hosepipe back into the exhaust and getting back into the car. I paced around the cottage and returned to him. I yanked out the hosepipe and opened the car door.

I tugged at him and he pulled away from me. He levered himself out of the car and replaced the hosepipe and got back into the car. I stood at the driver's door, unsure of what to do. I walked around to the passenger side. I thought of getting in and joining him. Would it make it all easier, to fly away together, and forget it all? I imagined the newspaper headlines: 'Lovers die in lovers' tryst'. I thought of our families going through our possessions, deciding what to keep; their shock and dismay. Paul was staring blankly ahead through the windscreen. His face was determined. His jaw set. Outside there was a haze and blankness. The year was advancing, so much green, lush velvet, even the weeds looked like they were colluding to appear as verdant as possible in the English summer. I felt weak and then something made me open the driver's door. He looked at me and I reached for his arm.

'Gerroff!'

'You can't do this.'

'What choice do I have?'

We stopped and looked at each other. I felt my heart beating like it would burst through my throat. I wanted his life to go on so much, for him and for me. He looked at the dashboard and not at me. I walked away again, back to the cottage. I looked at work that needed doing. We owed money to translators. I thought of them. I thought of him sitting in our car with the carbon monoxide pouring in. I could not blame him, but I didn't want it to end this way. I went back to the car. The birds were quiet and there was hardly a sound. We were living in this strange drama and there was no meaning to it at all. So why couldn't I say 'yes' and let it be? I tugged at the car door again. He threw me a vicious look.

'Get out of the car,' I said.

'No!'

'Please, I love you so much. I can't live without you. Please. Don't leave me here on my own, on this planet, without you.'

He looked at me blankly. 'I can't go on, I can't take it anymore.'

'Please, darling, please.'

He turned away and stared ahead. I walked back to the cottage. I was shaking and I wanted to give up, but I could not. I strode back to the car. I pulled the hosepipe out again and opened the door. He looked at me. I stomped away. I went into the cottage and it was silent and empty. I moved around, picking things up and putting them down. I sat down and flicked through a newspaper; everything was blurry and nothing made any sense.

I returned to the car. I could see his head through the car window as I entered the garage. I circled the car looking at him. He stared back at me. I took the pipe out. I was really angry now. I yanked the car door open and gripped his arm.

'Get out.'

'No.'

'I love you.'

He looked at me and then stared straight ahead. I went back to the cottage and then back to the garage.

Finally, exhaustion overcame us. I won. He pulled himself out of the car and let me take him back to the cottage. He returned to bed. I knew he was returning to his pain as well: the morphine his GP had given him only numbed the constant throbbing and tremors. In order to lessen the pain, he was taking over-the-counter medicine too: Nurofen, aspirin and paracetamol;

anything he could think of to make it go away. Had anyone seen our weird dance? Outside it was a peaceful summer's day. There was just the whisper of a breeze over the fields and drifting dandelion heads. Had the landlord watched us? The man was nowhere to be seen, probably holed up in his barn.

Paul flicked through computer and fishing magazines spread out on the bed. He told me that there had been a blue tit flying around the garage as he sat in the car with carbon monoxide pouring in. It was trapped. The garage doors were open but it had flown to the far side of the garage and into the window. Should he get out and save it? He decided it would alter its flight path and escape. It did.

Later he dragged himself to the office and tidied up the PC. He deleted files and checked it was working properly.

It was a perfect evening. The bats started to come out like fighter pilots from their hangars, turning and twisting as they scooped insects in the calm air. We were in the bedroom when we heard knocking at the back door. I went down. The landlord was standing in front of me.

'Is everything all right?'

'Everything's fine,' I lied.

'Paul all right?'

'He's bearing up.'

The landlord went; I felt relief. Paul was upstairs and alive. I deadheaded some of the roses and checked on the leaf mulch that I had started making in the autumn. I had placed the leaves in black bin bags in a shed in the garden. I opened the bags and peeked in. The leaves were still the same; they were not rotting down. I had read that it takes a long time to make a mulch. I was looking forward to the time when I would open those bags and find rich, crumbling soil. The time never came and I still wonder even now what became of my leaf mulch.

Tape 2: 31 July 2003: 12.26–13.07 continued

JA	So that gives us some idea of the severity of the pain. Anyway, I managed to get him out of the car and help him back into the house and that was how it was going. Then we'd have very positive times when we were talking constantly about the future. He wanted to get a larger satellite dish, things like that. At first I said, 'No, you can't have it,' and then two hours later I said, 'Yes, you can have it,' because I was buying him anything to make him stay alive.
DC Bosomworth	So is it fair to say that you stopped him on that occasion, do you think? If you hadn't been there, would he, do you think he would have done it?
JA	Yes, yes, yes he would; that was a serious attempt.
DC Bosomworth	And were there any others, Jill? I appreciate that it's upsetting you.
JA	Yes.
DC Bosomworth	I'd like to know.
JA	There were minor attempts, not as serious but he …
DC Bosomworth	What do you mean by a minor attempt?
JA	You know, he'd sort of say he was thinking about it and how much longer he could stay.

From a personality point of view, I can say that Paul was unpredictable.

If you asked Paul how he was he would always fill you in about some ailment he had. We know back in 1984, when he was twenty-four, after a failed relationship he attempted suicide once by cutting his wrists and secondly by taking an overdose of pills. This is all in the background, long, long before Jill comes on the scene. And his father described how he was suffering with a condition – ME/CFS – certainly by 1999 and that the condition, as you know, went on and on.

From the Defence's closing speech

Tape 2: 31 July 2003: 12.26–13.07 continued

DC Bosomworth	Right.
JA	And then I'd just talk him round. He was getting more and more disabled and he was using his feet to control the bath taps. His back had started cracking and I was saying, 'You've got to call me when you want to get out of the bath. I'll lift you up.'
DC Bosomworth	You've said that you cared for him for the last eight years.
JA	Yes.
DC Bosomworth	And you were his carer?
JA	Yes.
DC Bosomworth	How did this affect you, then? What did that entail for you?
JA	I was doing everything. At first he did what he could, but slowly, as his disability increased, I ended up taking care of the house, the garden, the car, the shopping and

cooking, going out into the outside world
and getting anything he needed, getting medication for him and . . .

DC Bosomworth Did you collect his medication?

JA Yes. I just completely altered my lifestyle.
When we first married, in the first part of our
relationship, he used to do housework.

DC Bosomworth Yeah.

JA He used to cook a meal for me at least once a
week. I thought I'd got my dream husband,
because he did housework and he liked
cooking.

June 2000

I was in a crumpled heap, snoozing; exhaustion struck. I had
been proofreading translations for the *British Medical Journal*,
checking and cross-referencing. I started suddenly: I could hear
him tiptoeing up the stairs. As my eyelids opened, a cup of tea
was placed next to me. He had always cooked, but whenever he
did I did not know what to expect.

On that evening he had left me as I catnapped. He combed
the kitchen. Food was low. He pulled out a packet of fish fingers from the deep freeze, peeled the batter off them and put
them in a dish. He found King Edward potatoes and cooked
them. He added slightly salted butter and full-cream milk and
whipped them into a fondant-like foam. He made a white sauce
and squeezed lemon into it. He placed the fish pie in the oven
and searched for vegetables in the fridge. He chopped some carrots and sliced green beans into long thin slivers and sautéed
them in a pan. He prepared a tray. He put a red tablemat on it,
went to the garden and picked a pink rose. He found a small

vase for the rose and placed it on the tray. He folded a dark green napkin and put a knife and fork on it. Then he went to the cupboard where we kept candles and bric-à-brac. He placed a single ivory candle in a holder and put that on the tray. He opened the oven, took out the pie and delicately scooped part of it onto a plate. He took the carrots and beans from the pan and laid them on the plate in a lattice crisscross. He went out into the garden again and picked herbs from the herb patch: parsley, thyme and rosemary. He washed and broke the herbs and scattered them over the pie and vegetables, adding a dab of butter. He put the pepper and salt shakers on the tray and placed a glass of water there, too. He lit the candle and then he climbed the stairs.

He watched as I ate. He had left some for himself downstairs. He would eat later. I finished and he took the tray and tucked the sheets up around my neck.

'How was it?' he asked.

'Lovely,' I replied.

'I'll make you a cup of tea,' he said and left the room.

I leaned back on the pillows. It tasted awful. How could I tell him? Too much lemon coupled with too many herbs. I smiled. He returned and we hugged.

And much later, he watched me put on my dressing gown and head down to the kitchen, where I would find total and utter devastation. As expected, every pot, pan and utensil in the entire kitchen was strewn over the work surfaces, and there was flour all over the floor with footprints running through it. By midnight it was all clean and tidy again. I would return to him and we would sleep skin to skin.

So, the issue in this case is, did Jill Anderson owe a duty of care to her husband? What does that mean?

She made it quite clear at interview that she was responsible for her husband's welfare. She accepted that she was his carer and that she had been his carer for eight years. No one can be expected to be on twenty-four-hour suicide watch; never going out of the door; never leaving someone on their own. Rather it was to take reasonable care of Paul Anderson. What would have been reasonable in this case?

It would be reasonable for a person who had a duty of care to pick up a telephone, dial '999' and summon medical assistance. It is not onerous and over-burdensome, it is the very least that a person ... could have done. And, had she done that simple act – she would have saved Paul Anderson's life.

The isolation, the inactivity and her exhaustion and stress were all the more reasons for seeking the assistance of others. And you take those matters into account and give them such weight as you think appropriate and proper; if you think they excuse her conduct, or if you think they provide adequate explanation so as to make her breach of duty excusable in terms such that it is not criminal.

From the Prosecution's closing speech

Tape 2: 31 July 2003: 12.26–13.07 continued

JA	In the last year he couldn't even make a cup of tea any more.
DC Bosomworth	Jill, did he actually dress himself?
JA	He would try to, then I'd come and help in the last six months of his life. I ran the bath for him and I laid out his clothes. He couldn't get into the cupboard to get the towels out or anything heavy. I'd put a towel on the back of the door for him and he managed to get into

his pyjamas but it was a struggle and very often I would come and do that for him. And that was devastating for him. He was a man and he didn't want to be dependent.

DC Bosomworth Oh, I can see that. Did you liaise with, for example, his GP on Paul's behalf?

JA Yes, I took over that aspect of his care.

DC Bosomworth When did you take that over?

JA There'd be a record somewhere where Paul made visits to his GP.

DC Bosomworth Right.

JA He had a series of toe infections where we called the doctors out because he was too ill to get to the surgery, tolerate the car journey and sit waiting for a doctor's appointment.

DC Bosomworth What causes toe infections?

JA He could hardly stand or sit. We've no idea.

DC Bosomworth For example, could Paul cut his own toe-nails?

JA I was going to cut them for him. He couldn't anymore.

DC Bosomworth I just want to show you a letter, Jill. It's exhibit AML1/5 from his medical records and it covers the fact that you were going to collect his prescriptions for him. If you recognize the letter, you can show your solicitor by all means.

JA Yes.

DC Bosomworth Thank you, and I think January 2002 is the date. I think that basically says that Paul's given you permission to speak to his GP on his behalf.

JA	Yes.
DC Bosomworth	I think that's a fair summary really, isn't it?
JA	Absolutely.
DC Bosomworth	And was it from that point that you actually did that?
JA	Yes. He would tell me what he wanted and I've made quite a few appointments with his GP.
DC Bosomworth	Yes.
JA	It should be recorded when I went to see the doctor. We discussed Paul's current condition. His GP did come unexpectedly one day to take some blood from Paul because we were having this constant debate with the medical profession. Paul said he had inflammation that was caused by his disease and they couldn't find any. The doctor said the tests are infallible but Paul said they are fallible and I must believe that.
DC Bosomworth	Okay.
JA	At some point in the future, he's going to be proven right, the tests are not infallible.
DC Bosomworth	Can you remember when you collected his last prescription?
JA	I think it was on the Monday before his death.
DC Bosomworth	Would that be on, round about, the 10th of July?
JA	Yes.
DC Bosomworth	And what would you have collected on that day?
JA	Morphine and Zopiclone.
DC Bosomworth	Right and what are they for, do you know?

JA	The Zopiclone's to help him sleep. He was in such pain that he rarely ever slept properly, and the morphine was for the pain.
DC Bosomworth	Right, and off the top of my head, I think there would be sixty morphine tablets which were given with the supply.
JA	Yes.
DC Bosomworth	And twenty-eight Zopiclone.
JA	Yes.
DC Bosomworth	Twenty-eight would be for a month's supply. Would you collect prescriptions on a monthly basis, then?
JA	Yes.
DC Bosomworth	How does it work?
JA	I just asked him when he needed some, I'd telephone the GP's surgery and then the GP issued it. It was a total relief because we'd had so many disagreements with doctors, but we'd finally found a GP who believed he was in serious pain and issued the medication without argument.
DC Bosomworth	OK, can you remember on how many occasions you collected these?
JA	No.
DC Bosomworth	Was that a standard prescription for Paul?
JA	Yes.
DC Bosomworth	Right, and how long had he been on that sort of standard prescription, any idea?
JA	About a year.
DC Bosomworth	Right. I'd say he's prescribed a month's supply. Would that be normal to get a month's supply at once?

JA	I'm assuming it is.
DC Bosomworth	Right and would Paul take all those?
JA	Yes, he self-medicated so he'd take them in the allocated time which is normally about a month and he did say that he was taking more than he should because he wanted to get rid of the pain.
DC Bosomworth	Would there be times he took less, for example, if he had a prescription of sixty morphine to last, say, for May? Would there be any chance he only took forty or would he stick to the dosage?
JA	I think he was pretty much sticking to the dosage.
DC Bosomworth	What I'm getting at, Jill, is, do you know if he was stockpiling any medication?
JA	I don't know, I just trusted him.
DC Bosomworth	Right. I'm only thinking it's possible that he could do this, that's all.
JA	And he was on the acute list, at risk.
DC Bosomworth	Yeah.
JA	I was on a twenty-four-hour suicide watch really, wasn't I? And I ... but I couldn't live my life like that. I just had to go with it each day and hope he'd make it through.

May 2003

I was in the lounge, sewing something, a hole in something, or a gap in a garment, or a split seam. I glanced at him as he wandered past me to the chair by the window at the side of the fireplace. It was a straight-back antique walnut chair, another

inheritance from my late grandmother's house. He would sit in
this chair occasionally and he did today. He looked out of the
window, into the stillness of the English countryside. He drank
the silence. He looked at me. Something was wrong: he knew
from my expression. I waited. He looked around the room and
there on the mantelpiece was an envelope. He slowly lifted himself up off the chair and reached for it. Inside was an invitation
to a wedding. One of my cousins was getting married in
September. She was a GP and well-travelled. She had visited us
when we first moved in and given us her kindness and support.
Now, at forty-five years old, she was getting married for the first
time to an engineer who built ships. The ceremony was near
Bath. It was going to be a lovely wedding and an enjoyable day.
He looked at me and, without words, we both thought of that
day. A simple service and then a meal in a country house with an
English garden. There were four cousins in my family and the
other three cousins had many children. We thought of children's
laughter and games. Everyone dressed up, polished and glossy
in their fine outfits.

How much we would like to go. He read and re-read the invitation. 'Jill and Paul, you are invited . . .' A pretty invitation,
ivory and gilt, he turned it around in his hands, felt the weight
of the embossed card. Then he put it back in the envelope and
returned it to the mantelpiece.

I continued sewing. 'Shall I send our apologies?' I said. I prepared another length of cotton for the needle. It was a pale, light
blue cloudless sky, heading towards summer and with it the long-
awaited warmth. The trees were almost in full leaf and renewal
was everywhere. The grass and the weeds grew in a fast, hungry
tangle. The birds were busy caring for their chicks.

'Yes.'

The silence remained between us. A fly buzzed somewhere in

the cottage. We liked the windows open; a bird had flown in once, a dunnock. He had caught it by throwing a hand towel over its shaking body and lifting the bundle out of the window. The bird was gone in a dash of brown, flapping its black, grey wings.

I wanted to hug him, but he was feverish, burning too much now to hold properly. In the end, the invitation would gather dust and then be thrown away. Later, much later, I would visit my cousin and finally meet her husband in Bath, but on my own.

Tape 2: 31 July 2003: 12.26–13.07 continued

DC Bosomworth Earlier you mentioned combing his hair?

JA Mmm.

DC Bosomworth Did you comb his hair for him?

JA I had to because his hair had grown long. He used to cut it himself but he stopped doing that because he couldn't lift his arms because he had frozen shoulders.

DC Bosomworth Right. I think he liked a tot of whisky occasionally?

JA Yes, he did. He was Scottish. He tried it for about three months as a painkiller. It didn't work, so he pretty much stopped drinking alcohol. He was hardly having any at all in the last year.

DC Bosomworth I tend to use alcohol, whisky, as an excuse for toothache.

JA Yes, he used to like his night out at the pub once a week when we first met.

DC Bosomworth But that stopped some time ago, didn't it?

JA	That stopped years ago. He used to play snooker. He was a very good snooker player and he loved it.
DC Bosomworth	You said that Paul had made a relationship between his illness and Gulf War Syndrome.
JA	Yes.
DC Bosomworth	Can you explain that to me a little bit?
JA	Because we were desperate for a cure for him, because the disease was part of our lives and because the medical profession couldn't come up with anything, we did a lot of reading and he made that connection some years ago. He frequently listened to shortwave radio and watched satellite television.
DC Bosomworth	Right. He wasn't in any services or had served in the Gulf or anything like that?
JA	No, he listened to discussion programmes a lot.
DC Bosomworth	I'm going to move on, Jill, distressing as it is for you.
JA	Yes.
DC Bosomworth	The 17th of July.
JA	We had an incredibly close relationship. I was monitoring him hourly.
DC Bosomworth	You were what, sorry?
JA	Monitoring him hourly. His moods, virtually the whole time I was ever with Paul he was in a very steady mood. That's how he was. He just woke up in the same mood and went to sleep in the same mood. He was very pleasant and peaceful, not negative. He was a

positive thinker, sharp wit, a good sense of humour, that's how he was most of the time. Now and again, completely understandably, he'd get frustrated and angry and lose his temper, explode. It was all over in ten, twenty, thirty minutes, that's how our relationship was. The weekend prior to his death he'd just been feeling more and more ill. He was starting to look very ill, it was dreadful. We spent the whole weekend crying together and I was begging him to stay alive. I was giving him every single reason I could think of and we both believed that he would recover. I kept saying, 'You're going to turn the corner. You're going to rise up. You will get well. I can feel it.' I suppose he had just had enough with the pain.

December 2002

He wanted to go downstairs, but he switched the television on in the bedroom instead. It rested on a pine cabinet that he was making for the TV, VCR and satellite unit. The cabinet had two shelves and a big space at the bottom for which he was going to make doors. He had started the year before. He felt frustrated: the illness was a straitjacket. He wanted to throw the TV out of the bedroom window. He was tired of looking at it. It was a small black television set that we had owned for many years. It did not have Ceefax, which really annoyed him. The second-hand television downstairs was broken and he often tried to fix it. Now he flicked through the channels and settled on a documentary about penguins. When the penguins went for a dip in the sea, seals came cruising for the penguin that was left behind and then ate it.

I heard him moving around and brought him a cup of tea. We exchanged our usual greetings. I was waiting for him; he knew that. He would have to come downstairs sooner or later. He made the effort and walked down the wooden slatted stairs that were his gateway to the lounge below. This room had the same dark green carpet as the bedroom, and a sofa with a pretty multicoloured throw. Opposite the sofa were two grey velvet armchairs and, between them, a low mahogany coffee table that had belonged to my grandmother. There were two windows in the same positions as the ones in the bedroom. One window had a view of the chestnut tree while the other looked out over the gravel yard to the fields beyond. In the far wall was the fire-place, which had a brass mantelpiece that glimmered with a roaring fire, burning away in the hearth. Underneath the logs there was a layer of coal to help the wood stay alight; our new coalman had informed Paul that the coal had been imported from South America as coal in England was now so scarce. The South American coal was flinty and charcoal-like in texture. It spat when it was lit. Shards of black coal would sporadically shoot out and hit the rug in front of the fire. A silk rug in dark purple, indigo and vermilion pinks, it was a gift from another family member. It depicted ancient battle scenes with men on horses brandishing swords and spears. Somehow the shards were never enough to ignite the rug, only tease it: the sparks usually went out before they reached the ground, like fireworks on bonfire night.

I had made the telephone calls I needed to make and was sit-ting on the sofa, staring into space. My cheeks felt hot, maybe because I had been for my walk, the one I always took on that day, or maybe it was because of sitting by the fire. There were many candles, ivory, scented, burning on the mantelpiece, which reflected back their light. On a side table there was a woven basket in which green apples, pomegranates and tangerines nestled together. On another side table there was a plate of figs and a box of Turkish delight and chocolates. A bowl of chestnuts was on the windowsill, waiting to be roasted over the fire. The room was decorated with holly, ivy and mistletoe picked from the hedgerows. The holly berries glowed, reflecting the fire. The room smelt musky with the foliage.

I was wearing a red velvet blouse and black trousers. I had put on the necklace he bought for me on the first Christmas we had shared together, and the bracelet; both gifts from the beginning of our relationship. I always wore them on that one day every year. I was also wearing some socks embroidered with reindeers. A friend of mine had sent them, the same friend who had also sent us two red felt hats covered in sparkles with white bobbles. He looked at the hats, which were under the tree.

'We'll wear them next year when you're well,' I said.

The nearby town of Ripon had enjoyed its usual annual fiasco. This year the tree in the main square, always imported from Norway, had been crooked and had to be removed to be replaced by a second crooked tree, which was then dispensed with and replaced by a third, almost straight tree. The population was reasonably happy.

The Christmas tree in the cottage almost reached up to the ceiling. It was a low ceiling with white-glossed wooden planks held up by oak beams painted black. When anyone over 6 feet tall came to visit, they often hit their head on these beams unless they bent down. As he was 5 feet 7 inches and I was 5 feet 3 inches, neither of us ever banged our head. He had wanted to go with me to get the tree from a local nursery, but on the day he was unable to go out. Getting the tree was one of his favourite things. It was decorated with lights and all kinds of ornaments, some handmade, some favourite old baubles, and tinsel, which ran through the tree and winked back through the lights. Under the tree, lay a heap of gifts of different sizes and shapes, encased in all colours of wrapping paper, bows, sparkles and ribbons.

I got up from the sofa and went to him. We kissed each other's cheeks, and then I reached under the tree and lifted out gifts. He felt queasy so I opened his gifts for him. He had a red fluffy dressing gown with blue piping all around the edge. 'Rupert Bear,' he said, as he sat on the sofa and ran his hands over the warm material. He smiled. He received the usual gifts of Scottish shortbread, chocolates, three pairs of socks, two cotton check shirts, pyjamas and a light green and sky blue country-style woollen sweater. It would keep the draught out if he wore it under his outdoor jacket. There were games, too, and books. There was a book for him from my family on the history of England, and a book about English wild flowers. He went back to bed. He felt too ill to watch me open my gifts; gifts that I had bought for myself, wrapped and pretended were from him. I bought what I wanted and informed him afterwards.

Later, I brought him his food. I cooked goose. It was the first time we had eaten it. It was a bit fatty and salty, but tasty, like sweet chicken. The plate was crammed with goose, mashed potatoes, roast potatoes, carrots, peas, beans, cauliflower, broccoli, stuffing, bread sauce and gravy. I propped up his pillows so that he could sit upright in bed with the tray of food on his lap. He picked at it. He couldn't eat all of it. I was eating downstairs. We had put our dining room table in the porch. The porch served a variety of uses, including a dining room. He had looked at the table, decked out with silver cutlery, wine glasses, napkins, candles and crackers.

I came to collect his plate and took it down to the kitchen, which was below the bathroom and a small bedroom that we had made into an office. He could not hear what I was doing but he knew I was busy tidying up, just like most of the rest of the country at that same moment. It was late afternoon and the light was fading. It had been a dry, crisp day with sunshine, plenty of light. The sky beyond the stark, snarled branches of the old chestnut tree was turning purple. He flicked through more channels. He listened to Verdi on his small CD player. This year he did not feel like watching the films we always watched together on this day. For the first time since we met, we skipped them. There was always next year, we supposed. The videos of *It's a Wonderful Life*, *Scrooge*, *Miracle on 34th Street* and *The Snowman*, could wait until next year. They could stand silent in the bottom section of the cabinet, with all the other videos he had accumulated.

Later in the evening, he came down again, slithering down the stairs. I had been up to the bedroom several times and had sat with him for a while. I had lain next to him and massaged him. He called a forehead massage a 'bear wood massage'. It was an evening ritual to go and visit each other. I had a game set up to play. There was a plastic cylinder with sticks interwoven inside it; marbles were placed on top of the sticks. Each player had to pull out a stick, trying not to disturb the marbles and let them fall to the bottom of the cylinder. He had a go. I had placed the cylinder on the low coffee table, but the angle needed to reach down to the sticks was agony for him. He could not twist his body into position and his arms flayed. So he gave up. He stood and watched as I played. We talked. He told me things, ideas and thoughts, and I listened. He revealed a secret that he had not told me before. He watched my face. I was fascinated. I offered him a glass of Scottish whisky, which had been his tipple, but he refused, as lately the smell of alcohol made him feel nauseous.

He stayed downstairs as long as he could, until the exhaustion and the jabbing pain took over. He returned to bed. He liked Christmas best when there was a large crowd of people gathered around the table. But this Christmas, it was a quiet one. Christmas had always been his favourite day.

Tape 2: 31 July 2003: 12.26–13.07 continued

DC Bosomworth   And do you think he came round a little bit from his thoughts that week?

JA   Yes, because all through this conversation I'm telling you about, crying and begging him to stay alive, he was dealing with it. He had an amazing sense of humour and we were talking about the future. He seemed quite talkative and we were making plans for his recovery.

DC Bosomworth   Right.

JA   Those were the events leading up to the Monday, Tuesday and Wednesday of that week. I couldn't distinguish them from any other week; they seemed to be normal, our normal routine.

DC Bosomworth   Yeah. Wednesday would be the 17th, I think.

JA   Yes. I just remember it was a bad weekend. Everything's so blurry now and I just know that it was a very emotional weekend for us.

DC Bosomworth   But he picked up a little bit from that weekend?

JA   Wanting to die wasn't always what we

discussed. It was only a small percentage that weekend. It must have been bad because we were both crying.

DC Bosomworth Right.

JA Ninety per cent of our conversation was about our future and he'd give me business advice from bed. He told me he was going to make all our bedroom furniture when he got well. We'd always talked about moving to Devon and then the south of France. We were talking again about all those plans.

DC Bosomworth Would it be fair to say that you were also giving him positive reasons to live?

JA Constantly, all the time.

DC Bosomworth I'm talking about this weekend.

JA Yes. He was a brilliant man and we had wonderful conversations. We'd talk about international events or friends and things people do. All the normal chit-chat of daily life. We laughed a lot because we liked laughing at the world, politicians and all the things you do laugh at.

Paul Anderson was an intelligent, mentally responsible person and he chose to end his life because of the chronic and relentless pain. Eight years of doctors; eight years of hospital visits and we have all been — you know what it is like. The queuing, the waiting, the anxiety over the results and so on. The medication, the hope that it works, and sadly if it does not. All the tests. He tried everything.

This was an impulsive overdose.

From the Defence's closing speech

Tape 3: 31 July 2003: 13.27–14.17

DC Bosomworth	I think to start with I'd like to say, Jill, that you've painted a good picture of Paul's illness.
JA	Yes.
DC Bosomworth	And I think we've got an indication of how much suffering he was in and how ill he was.
JA	Yes.
DC Bosomworth	What I propose to do now is move into more specifics.
JA	Yes.
DC Bosomworth	Because I'm anxious that you've had two interviews. This is your third.
JA	Yes.
DC Bosomworth	I thank you for your honesty and I appreciate it's upsetting for you but I'm going to ask you about details of the 17th. OK?
JA	Yes.
DC Bosomworth	You're aware that Police Officer Boulton was the first officer up there?
JA	Yes.
DC Bosomworth	And it's our duty to put a report to the coroner.
JA	Yes.
DC Bosomworth	Because that's usually why we attend when a doctor cannot sign a death certificate.
JA	Yes.
DC Bosomworth	I have a copy of that report here and paragraph two is the place of death, time and date and who the body was found by. I've spoken

to Police Officer Boulton because on here it says found at 10:00 hours on the 18th of the seventh by Jill Clare Anderson, wife, which is you.

JA   Yes.

DC Bosomworth   I'm a little concerned in that it says found at 10:00 hours when initially I was told by you that he was found at 5 a.m.

JA   That's when he turned blue, at 5 a.m.

DC Bosomworth   Right.

JA   It means no recovery. When he died it was about 9.30.

DC Bosomworth   Right, so you actually discovered him dead between 9 and 10 on the 18th, then?

JA   Yes.

Solicitor   Or you realized that he was.

JA   Yes.

DC Bosomworth   You've said in this interview that you discovered him between 5 and 6 and he was blue?

JA   Yes.

DC Bosomworth   And that you knew he was going to die?

JA   Yes.

DC Bosomworth   Did it not cross your mind, even at that point, that you should get an ambulance for him?

JA   Yes, I just didn't think, I didn't . . .

DC Bosomworth   Well, is there a reason why you didn't, bearing in mind, on two previous attempts you called an ambulance? Indeed, on one reported attempt you pulled a hose from the car exhaust pipe in order to stop him.

JA	Yes, and there have been lots of other attempts too.
DC Bosomworth	Is there any particular reason why this time you didn't call for some form of assistance?
JA	Because he'd gone blue.
DC Bosomworth	But, according to you, he still survived for three hours or thereabouts.
JA	I just felt he'd gone blue and that's it. I just felt that they wouldn't be able to bring him back.
DC Bosomworth	Was there no point throughout the evening, from say 7 p.m. onwards, that you felt you should call for an ambulance or at least a doctor?
JA	Not really, because we've done all this before and he'd make a recovery. I'd come back from Pateley Bridge and he promised me he was not going to do anything. It was so pleasant to see him asleep and he's done this before with whisky and a bit of extra medication.
DC Bosomworth	But on those previous occasions was there also a suicide note?
JA	Well, there was a whole series of these events. I was binning other suicide notes.
DC Bosomworth	Binning – you mean throwing them away?
JA	Yes.
DC Bosomworth	But you've certainly kept one other, haven't you?
JA	Yes, that was from, I can't remember, one of the events. It's so special that particular one because he had cut his hair and sellotaped it to the note. I decided to keep it.

DC Bosomworth Jill, I accept that you're saying that he self-medicated.

JA Yes.

DC Bosomworth I don't think I've a great problem with that, all right, to be frank with you.

JA Yes.

DC Bosomworth And that he drank his own whisky and he took his own medication and that his symptoms and his illness would make anybody miserable, wouldn't they? Or unhappy because you're in severe pain the majority of the time. I think you've said that he was in great pain?

JA Oh yes.

DC Bosomworth And at some point you'd had enough?

JA Yes.

DC Bosomworth Was it not the case this time that Paul had had enough and that you knew he'd had enough, and were, happy's not the right word, but we'll let him go this time?

JA I don't know because I wanted him to live more than anything else and I just hoped that he'd wake up again like he always did.

DC Bosomworth But you loved him dearly.

JA Very deeply, yes.

June 2001

He turned and he turned again – I watched. He was standing by the sink in Westowe Cottage. He had caught the first big one. It had weighed in at seven and a half pounds. He was grinning with satisfaction. He held the knife and the blade caught the sun.

Glittering. He had sharpened it earlier. He moved the rainbow trout round, its grey, blue-green scales still moist. He took the head off with one straight cut, then the tail and the fins. He lifted its silvery belly and sliced horizontally in one motion. He removed the innards and turned the trout round again. He made an incision down its spine and, with the knife, separated the bright pink flesh from the carcass, gently parting the flesh from the bones with even strokes. The job was done in a few minutes.

'How did you learn to do that?'

'I worked in a salmon factory in Scotland.' He placed two large trout fillets on a plate and covered them with a piece of paper towel. 'Flies,' he said.

I nodded. In the summer, we shared the cottage with creepy crawlies: it was impossible to stop them finding a way in. When I entered the storage shed in the winter, I always looked up at the ceiling because, among the old oak rafters, there was always an array of pupae, butterflies and moths, hanging, motionless, waiting. We had found a pupa in soil at Rose Cottage so we had taken it back to our bedroom and placed it in a glass tank on our windowsill to see if it would hatch, but it never did as we had not created the right conditions.

He cleared up the waste bits of fish and wrapped them in a sheet of newspaper, then took the package into the lounge to put onto the open fire, which was low in the hearth. In the summer we kept a low fire for the evenings. I scrubbed the new potatoes under the sink tap, their tender skins rubbing off to reveal crunchy bulbous white. I had a pan boiling on the stove and dropped the potatoes into it. Slices of lemon and fresh shelled peas were on a plate nearby. I would steam the trout with butter in a little while and garnish the plate with parsley gathered from the herb patch, which was in a rectangular bed just outside the kitchen window. A vole lived in the wall bordering the herbs. As

I stood at the sink I often watched it dash through the herbs. In winter it moved even faster.

Tape 3: 31 July 2003: 13.27–14.17 continued

DC Bosomworth	And you didn't like to see him suffering.
JA	Well, no one does. That's why I went and got medication for him.
DC Bosomworth	And really this was the ultimate release for him.
JA	I wanted him to live and I was going to promise to get laser treatment for his arms.
DC Bosomworth	Is there anything you want to ask, Mike, just on this bit here?
DC Richardson	It's just concerning me a bit, Jill. Obviously I've been taking notes as this has been going on.
JA	Yes.
DC Richardson	And you've mentioned when you came back to the house and he said the words, or words to the effect of 'sorry I've taken too much' and you weren't sure or you were in two minds, you've mentioned, whether he had or hadn't, is that right?
JA	Yes, and he had said that to me before anyway.
DC Richardson	OK.
JA	This was an ongoing event for us unfortunately.
DC Richardson	There's a bit of a difference in this respect in that he's sleeping peacefully.

JA	Yes.
DC Richardson	As opposed to normal occasions when this might have happened.
JA	He went through bouts where he could get sleep relief and sleep peacefully and that was always a very great pleasure for me. Chronic Fatigue Syndrome causes problems with regard to being able to sleep, so when he did sleep I let him sleep.
DC Richardson	We've just got unusual aspects in this, on this particular day, insomuch as we've spoken about the whisky, which was unusual for this day. He has mentioned words to the effect of 'sorry I've taken too much', there is a note and he's sleeping peacefully. There's sort of four unusual circumstances on this occasion and it still left you in two minds.
JA	Yes, because we'd had this sequence of events before where he'd had whisky. He'd had a little too much medication and I was very exhausted as well and emotionally stressed and I don't think I was thinking straight that night. I just saw him asleep and I thought just let him sleep it off. That was the sequence of events that had always occurred and when he woke up at 2 a.m. I just thought, Oh there isn't a problem, and I popped his earpiece back in for him.
DC Richardson	We've also spoken about something else that was unusual, what you described as this 'bad weekend' with discussions and suicidal thoughts before that.

JA	Yes.
DC Richardson	I appreciate your exhausted state of mind as well.
JA	Yes.
DC Richardson	But I'm trying to paint a picture of some things that were more unusual than normal in Paul's life on this evening when he has mentioned to you that he has taken too much. I'm trying to work out your thinking at that point and the fact that – as a carer for Paul – even if you're in two minds, wouldn't you have considered calling for medical assistance whether he had or hadn't taken anything?
JA	Can I have a word with my solicitor, please?
DC Richardson	OK certainly. We're going to stop the interview for legal advice.

March 2001

He had been awake all night. We had to do something. I called the doctor. I was watering seedlings, many trays of them, when she came. She looked at them as she entered the cottage: they were on the porch windowsills.

'Gardening a bit of a passion, is it?' she said airily, as she glided past me and up the stairs. I had socks on, but no slippers. As we climbed the stairs she turned to me and said, 'Do you sew?'

'No, not much.'

'Good,' she said, 'there won't be any pins in the carpet.'

She seemed sharp and brittle. I wondered why. We had had a variety of debates with her about the usual issues, such as the existence of CFS. We reached the top of the stairs and she entered the bedroom ahead of me. She began her examination.

'Do you ever get up?' she asked him.

'Yes,' he said, 'as much as I can.'

Her manner felt unsympathetic as she said, 'Can't you walk down the lane every day?'

'No,' he replied, 'I would if I could. Have you ever had flu?' She nodded.

'Well times it by ten.'

She stuck a swab into his mouth. 'I'll check you for diabetes.' She removed the swab, shook it and looked at it. 'You're not diabetic,' she said.

He was getting more and more impatient. He was stirring in bed and his eyebrows were twitching. Her face was impassive. Perhaps she had seen a child with terminal cancer that morning, I thought.

'Can you test me for hepatitis?' he asked.

She stuck a needle in his arm and took some blood.

'Can we have an appointment to go to Newcastle General? There's an expert based there. I found him on the Internet,' I asked.

She said she would write the letter. She looked around the bedroom and touched the mattress on the bed. 'A bit squishy,' she said.

I could feel blood rising in me: she did not believe us. I took her downstairs and led her out of the cottage to her car. She got in and I watched. The engine would not start. She got out and approached me.

'I've run out of petrol.'

We looked at each other.

'I'll go to the village and get some petrol for you,' I said.

We went together. She handed her petrol can to me. I made

the journey quickly. I suppose she had had a break from routine. When I handed the full petrol can back to her, our eyes met and somehow I had empathy for her as one woman to another. I had to forgive her. I knew that, and so did Paul. Later in the year, we changed our GP to the head of the practice, who was considered to be the best doctor in the area. He was kind to Paul, even though we suspected he did not believe CFS existed.

Later in the day, I went up to see Paul and he was lying flat on his back as usual. He turned to me and said, 'I'm a pin cushion.'

She was a lady of good character and however carefully and under-standing the officers who carried out the interrogation, then you may think it was something entirely alien for her – and you may think frightening – she must have thought about his fatal overdose every day and no doubt still thinks about it.

She did what most of us could not perhaps do; consciously let the one she loved go and put her wishes in second place. You may think it was for her sake that she was saying that she had wished she had called an ambulance. She respected his wish to choose to die with dignity in his own home, not in a sterile bed in hospital, and to end the relentless pain he had endured over the years. She made the sacrifice and gave up – you may think – part of her life in letting him go, and you may conclude – it is a matter for you – that she acted with a rare courage.

From the Defence's closing speech

Tape 3: 31 July 2003: 13.27–14.17 continued

DC Bosomworth   We've had a brief break in this interview, Jill, in order for you to consult your solicitor. Is that correct?

JA	Yes.
DC Bosomworth	And we haven't discussed this with you in that break?
JA	No.
DC Bosomworth	I'm going to remind you again of the caution.
DC Richardson	I was asking about circumstances. You remember the question?
JA	It's the hardest thing for me. I've just lost my best friend, and I wanted him to live and, in hindsight, I've got to live with it for the rest of my life. I wish I'd called the ambulance in hindsight but I didn't. I don't know why and that's how it was. I just thought he was going to sleep it off. When he woke up at 2 a.m., it had all happened before. I know it sounds like a strange set of circumstances to wish someone . . . with the pills and the note and sleeping. It had all happened before in our lives, like on the weekend before; suicide was now part of our language. I didn't call an ambulance because I just didn't think it would ever happen. He'd been through it so many times before and he always came back. He was always alive.
DC Richardson	You always did something to stop him. You've told us about taking the hosepipe from the car.
JA	Oh yes.
DC Richardson	You've made calls to the hospital and got medical assistance.
JA	Yes.

DC Richardson	Before, on previous attempts.
JA	Yes.
DC Richardson	Didn't this experience or these experiences make you think about erring on the side of caution when he said that he'd taken something and the circumstances were building up to that?
JA	He'd done it before. Cases that I haven't even recorded on the tape or reported because there was no point. He always woke up and so I was facing a repeat set of scenarios. The other times when he took mouse poison and had blue stains all over his mouth. The Zopiclone was making him walk into the wardrobes and he was hallucinating. I don't know what the difference was because these events were happening on a continuous basis and we were living with it. What has probably come out incorrectly is that this was not a big part of our lives.

January 1996

We crunched through the snow; it was crisp and our feet tingled. We were walking on the surface of the moon, or that's what it felt like in our imaginations. We held hands together so we were less likely to slip. The snow had been falling all day. The television news reports stated that the whole country had come to a standstill.

By 2 p.m. it was obvious that nothing much was going to happen in the commercial world. We shut down our computers and put the answering machine on, delighting in our freedom, feeling like seven-year-olds again. We raced around our flat in Pateley Bridge, covering ourselves in wool and waterproofs. We were full of anticipation of our expedition into the snow. We kept looking out of the windows. Through the fast-falling snow, we could see that the entire landscape had changed. The rocky outcrops high on the moors were white. The best thing was the silence of our town, as all the traffic and human noise had come completely and utterly to a halt.

We set off into the muffling snow, grasping each other as we made our way excitedly down the High Street. All the shops were closed, and there was no one around at all. Our faces glowed, but mine more than his. The objective for this journey was to visit a badger sett that was further along the River Nidd, which stretched through Pateley Bridge. We thought that the snow would make the badgers' footprints more visible. Our theory was that the snowstorm might make these nocturnal creatures come up out of their underground home to forage, so we might catch sight of them.

As we stamped through the snow, our woollen-gloved hands were clasped together as if we were one. He talked about survival and I listened. It was all common sense: stay dry, find shelter, find water and find food; how to make an igloo. We talked about the life of an Eskimo, what it must be like, how when they got very, very old and infirm the elders would walk out into the snow and not come back. How warm an igloo could be, with furs from polar bears and seals. We did not think badgers had ever been hunted and eaten – we were not sure.

We walked on. The snow fell abundantly. We crossed over the bridge to the other side of the river. On the left bank there was a walkers' path that was normally well marked, but what was exciting today was that the path and its boundaries had disappeared. We looked back at the town of grey stone, which was a blanket of white. Snow fell into our eyes and all around us. We wiped the wet from our faces and crunched on. How we adored disruption to routine, something different from the usual.

In another fifteen minutes or so, we both looked like snowmen, covered from head to foot with petals of ice. We blinked at each other and grinned. We sang and danced. Snow excited us. It was its indifference to anything that we both liked, the way snow covered the landscape and made it disappear and become bumps and bobbles, making us not quite sure where the paths were anymore. I made a snowball and threw it at him; he returned fire. We bounced along, laughing, thinking of maybe seeing a badger.

We reached the badger sett, but nothing moved. The snowfall had eased and there was a settling of the atmosphere into a comforting silence. There were no footprints. We stood and breathed in the soft kiss of the white flakes drifting down all around us. We could hardly make out the trees, fields or the moors – or the way home. We decided that the badgers were sensible, like all the other creatures, and were bunkered in underground beneath our feet, resting, hopefully with a stash of food to see them through this snow. Perhaps they had fires blazing and were telling their children ancient legends of King Arthur and his knights, and the badger children were squished up close to their parents wrapped in their black and white fur, entwined, warm until the storm subsided.

We turned back. The snow was much thicker now and reached above our boot tops, climbing up to our knees. It was harder to see, harder to walk, and our noses were bright red from the cold. We smiled at each other, the quest, unfulfilled but attempted, and the fight to return. Maybe the drift would reach our waists soon. Maybe we would take a wrong turn and fall down a crevice. No one would find us until we were frozen corpses, our eyes wide open and fixed.

We giggled and gripped each other, wove our woollen fingers together. We would pull each other out of this storm. The town was a screen of white before us. We thought of the crevice and the search-and-rescue team. Would they look for us, would they know, how would they know?

We held on tighter to each other. The snow was 2 feet deep in some places and the path was full of ditches. One foot in the wrong place could be disaster. The river had taken lives before. We tried to judge how close we were to its swirling, black ice water, begging us to make a mistake and fall in. We searched for our bearings and moved on, slowly through the drift. It was getting colder but the falling snow was slowing. We walked in each other's footsteps. He led, I followed and slowly but surely the town started to reach us from its shadows, the grey, blue, black from behind the veil of the white snow.

We walked up the centre of the High Street; there were no cars. The light was fading and the street lamps were not yet on, but the lights from the homes above the shops illuminated the gloom. We got home and ran a bath, jumping in together, our bright, pink, red flesh squashed into the tub. We lit candles all around us and rubbed oil and soap into each other's bodies, making bubbles together. We got out, wrapped towels around each other and drank brandy.

That night we slept deeply and dreamed of the badgers at home in their sett, snuffling and content, black and white. They would come out into a new world of pure, white virgin snow above ground, untouched. The snow continued to fall overnight and when we woke it was even deeper; nothing moved.

Tape 3: 31 July 2003: 13.27–14.17 continued

JA	It's just another part of our lives and most of the conversation was positive. The next thing I was going to buy for him was a larger satellite dish and we'd been talking about that that morning. Prior to that he described how he was going to make a casket to put the bed linen in. We had so many plans. I didn't take it all in. I've got the rest of my life to wonder should I have made the call and I didn't, so I've got to live with that now.
DC Richardson	I appreciate what you're talking about now, but we've got to look at what you were thinking of. Your thought process at the time. I appreciate you're talking about hindsight and everything.
JA	Right, the thought process was this, I was not involved at all in how much medication he'd taken, he did that all himself.
DC Richardson	He woke up at 2 a.m., didn't he?
JA	Yes.
DC Richardson	And you've mentioned previously that you said or you thought he hadn't taken too much?
JA	That's right.
DC Richardson	And great.
JA	That's right, I had no idea because the medication was always stacked up at the side of the bed. I never looked at it. I had too many other things to do.

DC Richardson	So when he did wake up? Was it two o'clock?
JA	Yes.
DC Richardson	How did you feel?
JA	Great. Normal. I just popped his earpiece in for him.
DC Richardson	So, you did mention that you thought he hadn't taken too much.
JA	That's right.
DC Richardson	Which would insinuate that initially you thought he had.
JA	I had to go with my instincts and what had happened before. This time it seemed like all the other times. He was asleep and I thought let him sleep it off. He's had a few too many and this all happened before. I don't know what was going on in my head.
DC Richardson	Jill, did it come to a point where you thought that he may have taken something and you were in two minds? He was in so much pain and you were so emotionally and physically exhausted yourself that you thought it was probably for the best if he passed away peacefully with you at that time.
JA	No. I wanted him to live more than anything else. I was just in such total shock when you all came round to the house. I just didn't know what I was saying but I just thought he was going to make it because he had before and that's it. I don't like it because he's not here and all I want is to hear his voice again and all the conversations we were having, even up to the last few days. I know it sounds

like the focus is on dying but there were so
many other positive things that we were talking about and he had so much to live for and
he'd just got unlucky. He got a virus and a
terrible disease that we were dealing with.
You just carry on and that was our attitude.

July 1998

We set out that day for Eavestone Lake. It was summer again.
We had our swimming costumes with us. He led, I followed,
and then we reversed positions as we stepped carefully down
the steep path that descended the wooded hill to the lake. In
spring this area was covered in deep pink, red and white rho-
dodendrons. We reached the lake and checked on the Canada
geese. They had a nest on an islet. We would watch them each
year. They had gone now. He usually had his bird book and
binoculars with him. We shared them, stopping to watch the
moorhens hugging the banks, dipping in and out of the reeds,
fast, fussy, busy birds. There were tufted ducks and ruddy
ducks meandering, grazing and arguing.

The lake rippled like fairy lights as we walked around it. We
noted our favourite stopping points. There was a rocky outcrop
that we liked to climb sometimes; it had a mossy tabletop. We
walked on by. Pines rose on all sides, mixed with oaks, beech
and yew, all in a jumble. It seemed that when we were at the
edge of the lake, all evil was shut out and this place possessed
the comfort of a womb. There was no main road nearby and the
only sound was the dense rustling of a breeze. The only buzz
was the insects, with their flight paths at every level, radar on
the alert, thoroughfares, roads and byways in the sky.
Dragonflies darted and drifted.

We joked about the time when we were sitting on the bank, using our waterproof trousers as a picnic blanket. The ground seemed to be moving around us. On close inspection we realized we were surrounded by baby frogs, hundreds of them in the wild grass.

We got to the far end of the lake. The ground was reasonably flat there, and Paul stripped off to his trunks and went into the water. He made me think of a human eel and I called him 'Skinny Eel'. The water was sharp and cold. I saw him shiver. There was a network of tangled reeds. He negotiated his way out of them into deeper depths and went under a few times to explore. He swam, paddling forwards and backwards.

Then the moment came. It was a shock. He was sinking under. I got up and went to the edge of the bank and shouted, 'Are you all right?' The water was taking him down. He gasped. His eyes rolled. I started to wade in. I saw him go under, and then he reappeared and lunged forwards. He had found solid ground and began to wade to me. I grabbed hold of him, pulled him to the bank and helped him onto land. It had all happened so fast; in seconds.

He never swam again. He could only remember the pleasure of diving. He said that if he dived he would never come back up. Swimming belonged with tennis, only a memory, our rackets in the outside shed covered in dust, kept just in case.

Tape 3: 31 July 2003: 13.27–14.17 continued

DC Richardson   You've mentioned that you're sure that he was blue between 5 and 6 and you thought to yourself, 'He's done it this time.' What did you mean by that?

JA	This whole thing that happened was not pre-meditated in any shape or form by me. If I'd come in and seen he obviously had taken a lot I would have pulled it all out of his mouth and made him vomit it up, but I didn't. I was not there.
DC Richardson	Who made the decision?
JA	And I couldn't watch him twenty-four hours a day, so when he turned blue I knew there was no recovery.
DC Richardson	At that point though, Jill, you've made a decision that he wasn't going to get better. Is that correct?
JA	I don't know, I can't tell you what was in my head. I was just a mess, as you can imagine, because he was still asleep and I just didn't know.
DC Richardson	Right, at that point, when he had gone blue, it's a decision that you took not to call for medical assistance, knowing that there was a problem.
JA	Yes.
DC Richardson	Why was that?
JA	Well, I don't know. I've never read any-thing about morphine. I've only read about morphine when I've purchased it as a pain-killer. I don't know what it does if someone takes too much. I've no idea. I don't know what I was thinking. If they tried to revive him, would he end up as a vegetable in a coma?
DC Richardson	I would suggest that between 5 and 6 when

	you discovered him turning blue that that was the point, if not before, to call for medical assistance. You seem to have made that decision on the basis of something that you read. Do you think you were the best-qualified person to make the decision not to call for medical assistance?
JA	No, of course not, and, in hindsight, I wish I'd made the call. I didn't and I've got to live with that for the rest of my life.
DC Richardson	I appreciate it's a difficult time and there's a lot of muddle.
JA	Yes.
DC Richardson	But it would help to know your state of mind and your thought process at the time when you've mentioned the words 'I've taken too much' and the time when he was discovered blue.
JA	Right, he'd said that he'd taken too much before and recovered.
DC Richardson	Did you make any telephone calls at all?
JA	Well, it was 5 or 6 in the morning, so no.
DC Richardson	Had you made any telephone calls after he'd told you, 'Sorry, I've taken too much,' or words to that effect?
JA	No.
DC Richardson	So from that point you made no telephone calls until you contacted the doctor. Is that a fair statement?
JA	That's right.
DC Bosomworth	Right, a couple more questions that you're not going to like but nevertheless I'm going

	to ask them. You've mentioned bankruptcy with Paul or Paul was bankrupt.
JA	Yes.
DC Bosomworth	And would anybody benefit from Paul's death?
JA	No.
DC Bosomworth	Are there any insurance policies regarding Paul?
JA	Definitely not. We put everything in my name. He had his own bank account, so no one benefited from his death at all.
DC Bosomworth	Do you believe that now he is free from all his pain?
JA	I want him to be with me so I'm selfish and that's how you feel about the one you love the most. I don't like to think about it. I just wish he'd never got a virus.

Then at 5, she checks him and he has gone blue. What does she do? The Prosecution say that she should have done the simple thing. Pick up the phone. Well the simple thing she did was to pick his favourite flowers, clean the house and call the doctor. Do you think for a moment that she believed he wanted to come round from this?

From the Defence's closing speech

Tape 3: 31 July 2003: 13.27–14.17 continued

DC Bosomworth	Right, can I ask you why you hoovered the home?
JA	When I cleaned the house he was dead. No

one could do anything and there was no
point in calling the GP. I thought, why dis-
rupt another human being's day? My
husband's dead and no one can do anything
about it. I wanted a few hours to myself with
him, because I knew the GP would come and
certify him.

Solicitor	I think the question was why you hoovered up.
JA	Oh yes, sorry, I just cleaned the house because I couldn't think of anything else to do. I wanted it to be neat and tidy for when the GP came and that's it. I didn't remove anything, I just did housework.
DC Bosomworth	Did Paul feel the cold particularly or not?
JA	No, I kept the house warm for him. We loved the windows open. We always had the windows open in summer.
DC Bosomworth	Was there any reason for the heat being on in the bedroom?
JA	I didn't know that it was.
DC Bosomworth	Well, according to Police Officer Boulton the bedroom was hot and the heat was turned on.
JA	In the mornings the water heater comes on and there was a radiator in the bedroom so that's the reason it was on. It was an automatic water heater timer so I wouldn't have even noticed the water heater coming on that day.
DC Bosomworth	And what time would that turn on then?
JA	I don't know. I think it's between 7 and 9 or something like that at the moment.
DC Bosomworth	It goes off at 9 then, does it?

JA	Yes, something like that. It's very warm with clocks coming on all the time. I don't keep a track of it. I just keep the cottage comfortable for both of us.
DC Bosomworth	I haven't made many notes in this interview because I've been asking the questions.
JA	Yes.
DC Bosomworth	But one line I've written down, 'I cried and begged him to stay alive,' which I think was in relation to the hosepipe incident.
JA	Yes.
DC Bosomworth	With the car.
JA	Yes.
DC Bosomworth	Cried and begged him to stay alive, and you said that you're selfish and you wanted him to live.
JA	Yes.
DC Bosomworth	But on this last attempt you did nothing, so far as I can see, to assist him in living.
JA	He'd done it before and I think that was just my reasoning; that we'd been going through this experience for some time and I loved him. I suppose I just wasn't thinking straight about everything.
DC Richardson	You mentioned about morphine and you don't really know the effects of . . .
JA	No I don't.
DC Richardson	Am I right in thinking that you assumed that that's the cause of his death?
JA	I don't know. I don't know what caused his death at all. It's just that he was on morphine and I've no idea what was in his drawer.

DC Richardson	You mentioned that he self-medicated.
JA	And he had loads of medication left over from other medications he had tried in the past. He was taking a lot of medication.
DC Richardson	Jill, that evening, or the evening before Paul took his life, did you in any way discuss taking his life?
JA	No.
DC Richardson	Right, did you assist him in any way?
JA	No.
DC Richardson	Were you there when he took the tablets?
JA	No.
DC Richardson	You weren't. When I say there, I mean physically there, I don't mean downstairs.
DC Bosomworth	Did you see him?
JA	I didn't see him.

Another fact you may want to consider, is whether Paul Anderson was in fact competent to take a rational decision. There is in English law a presumption of competence. Every person is presumed to be competent unless the presumption is displaced. And sometimes, it does not take much to displace it. If someone behaves irrationally, or if they seem to be behaving in a peculiar way, you may properly conclude that the person is not competent, not competent enough to make a normal decision.

The Prosecution case is, in any event, Paul Anderson was not competent to take a decision to end his own life and we, on that aspect of the case, would invite you to consider the position in which he found himself. In the last few months of his life it appears he was virtually bedridden. No visitors. No social life. Estranged from his family and in pain from his illness. He was being subjected to abnormal stresses which would be liable to cause him to act in an irrational fashion and do odd things which he would not normally contemplate. The medical opinion was that there was nothing physically wrong with him. Paul Anderson had not submitted himself for psychiatric assessment and you may think that his condition cried out for psychiatric assessment and treatment. It is not rational to commit suicide rather than seek a psychiatric assessment. A psychiatric assessment, in any view, is better than death.

From the Prosecution's closing speech

PART III

Tape 4: 25 January 2004: 11.17–11.59

DC Bosomworth   There's going to be a couple of interviews at least today, Jill, and the first part, the first bit I actually want to cover, is Paul's family. You were married to Paul Anderson, yes?

JA   Yes.

DC Bosomworth   And he obviously had family.

JA   Yes.

DC Bosomworth   But, at the time of his death, you obviously knew these people existed?

JA   Yes, I did.

DC Bosomworth   Was there any particular reason you didn't contact the family regarding Paul's death or indeed ask us to do so on your behalf?

JA   Yes, there was.

DC Bosomworth   Would you like to tell me what the reason was?

JA   Paul asked me that if anything ever happened to him I was to have no further contact with his family.

DC Bosomworth   Do we know why that was?

JA   Yes, we'd kept in touch with them continuously until about the year 2000. We only moved to Yorkshire to be close to family, to be close to my mother in Ilkley and to be close to his family in Gretna. The

	intention was to spend lots of time with them.
DC Bosomworth	Right.
JA	We had 100 per cent support from his mother. I had the most fantastic mother-in-law. She came to visit us and we had the most wonderful day. She believed Paul was physically ill and she told me that she wasn't well. She had emphysema and angina, and her parting words to me were, 'I can die happy now, Jill, because I know you and Paul are together.'
DC Bosomworth	But is it fair to say the rift was through Paul's illness and the family's disbelief that he was physically ill?
JA	Yes.
DC Bosomworth	Is that it in a nutshell?
JA	That's it in a nutshell.
DC Bosomworth	And, I suppose, in some ways, Paul felt betrayed by that.
JA	Yes.
DC Bosomworth	You'll be aware we've spoken to members of the family.
JA	Yes.
DC Bosomworth	I mean we've disclosed that to your solicitor.
JA	Yes.
DC Bosomworth	Paul's dad states that he was happy when Paul met you.
JA	Yes.
DC Bosomworth	Did he ever express that to you?
JA	Yes, we used to have lovely times with him.
DC Bosomworth	And you and Paul set up a translations business.

JA	At that time it was Anderson Translations.
DC Bosomworth	Right, I was just going to ask, was it ever called anything else?
JA	Yes. We worked from 1995 to 1998 and went bankrupt because of his illness.
DC Bosomworth	So it was called what to start with?
JA	Anderson Translation Services.
DC Bosomworth	Right and you changed its name because of the bankruptcy.
JA	Yes.

April 1998

Paul was sitting in the Official Receiver's office in Leeds. I sat in a waiting room outside, but I could see him talking through a glass window that divided us. We had lugged our business files and paperwork up three flights of stairs to get here. I noticed he was having difficulty with his arms so I carried as much as I could. The building was another unexceptional red-brick block in the centre of Leeds.

The Receiver, who was in her late thirties, was looking at him intently. She had welcomed us when we got there. She spoke quietly and had kind eyes. We had filed for bankruptcy months ago at Harrogate County Court. We had sat with a group of people of all ages who were, like us, fighting back tears.

Now the day we both dreaded had arrived. 'Oh the cruelty of it all,' he said as we dressed together that morning at Rose Cottage. Outside, it was an average day, neither cold nor hot. The sky was overcast. We had worked for weeks on closing down Anderson Translation Services, paying off each individual translator to whom we owed money. Now we were only in debt to the high street banks, and it was spread out in small sums to each of them. We had worked hard on the paperwork and everything was neatly displayed in lever-arch files, numerically and in order. It was how he had wanted it. If we had to file for bankruptcy then we had to do it professionally. I did not argue with him. I just followed his instructions because they made sense.

He was not in her office for long and when he came out he looked relieved. It was over. We had declared ourselves bankrupt and we had accepted responsibility. We were both determined to start again somehow and soon. He told me the conversation that he had had with her. She had been sympathetic and fully understood our situation. She hoped he would get well again.

We lugged the files back down the stairs, back out onto the street. We were crushed.

I said to him, 'We'll start again, somehow.'

A homeless person came up to us. He was grubby and unshaven, with yellowish skin: 'Have you got any change?'

'We've just gone bankrupt,' we echoed each other.

He curled his lip and shrugged.

'Here, mate.' Paul dug into his pocket and gave the man some change.

He walked away.

'What did you do that for?' I said.

'Had to, that's all.'

The streets of Leeds were filled with people rushing. Lunchtime. City girls in low heels and suits. City men in ties and suits. Workers, cleaners, traders, shoppers, students, unemployed people and truants all streamed relentlessly around us.

'Do you want to do anything here?'

'No,' he said.

We went back to Rose Cottage and talked about starting again.

Tape 4: 25 January 2004: 11.17–11.59 continued

JA	But we had to stop it and restart it.
Solicitor	So you started again.
JA	Yes, I started again.
DC Bosomworth	I appreciate the reason for changing the name of the business was basically financial difficulties.
JA	Yes.
DC Bosomworth	Right. Your marriage to Paul.
JA	It was in London. We just wanted it to be very simple. It was a registry office and my mother and Frank, my stepfather, my brother and his then girlfriend and one of my husband's sisters, her partner and her son attended. The reason that we kept it small was because his mother wasn't very well. We explained that to them and said we were going to do a large ceremony when we got to Yorkshire.

Jill's account – the Prosecution do not doubt it for a moment – indeed they rely upon it. They rely upon her openness, honesty, frankness in accurately describing what happened.

You have heard something of her CV. Intelligent, outgoing, hard-working, never been in trouble with the police. From the time she married him, his health began to deteriorate. She gave up her job, her independence and her freedom to become his business partner. He was the brains; he was the translator; she was the administrator and then, to become his housekeeper, his nurse and his companion. She fought his battles with the doctors and with his own disbelieving family.

Inevitably, he and she cut themselves off from his family because of his obsession with his illness and her desire to support him all the way.

From the Defence's closing speech

Tape 4: 25 January 2004: 11.17–11.59 continued

DC Bosomworth	Did you have a ceremony in Yorkshire then?
JA	No, he got too ill.
DC Bosomworth	And his mother died.
JA	Yes.
DC Bosomworth	And you and Paul went up to the funeral.
JA	Yes. He collapsed twice and was sick in the church. We couldn't believe his family's attitude. We kept on saying that he was physically ill. I was very upset. I remember sitting downstairs in his sister's house and one of his nephews walked into the room and said, 'Oh I hope I don't end up like that.'
DC Bosomworth	Did you and Paul argue at the funeral or the wake afterwards?
JA	I don't recall us having any argument that day whatsoever. I was completely supportive of him. He was very physically ill. I loved every hair and molecule of him and I devoted my life to trying to save his life for years.
DC Bosomworth	I believe around Christmas 1999, the family wanted to come and visit Paul.
JA	That's right.

DC Bosomworth	You stopped them visiting him.
JA	Yes, I said to his father, 'Would you mind if we book it provisionally? Paul has Irritable Bowel Syndrome and he's going to the toilet fifteen times a day.' There was only one toilet in the cottage and I was thinking of them. How would they go to the toilet if he needed to go to the toilet? It was very uncomfortable because he had diarrhoea and I thought it was unfair to them to come to the cottage and have to experience that. I said 'Would you mind if we book it provisionally?' and when he replied he exploded.
DC Bosomworth	Who?
JA	His father. I was very polite. After his mother died, I had given his father counselling support and told him, you are our hero, we love you, we need you, you and Isla were the most beautiful couple. We are so proud of you, meaning that he was carrying on after her death. We just gave him such kind words. Paul made three or four attempts to mend the rift. He called his father. I remember him on the phone saying to his father, 'Can we sort this out, Dad?' Paul's blood pressure kept on dropping and I was terribly worried about him. So I went to see his GP. We talked in depth for nearly an hour. He told me that Paul was making up Chronic Fatigue Syndrome, that it was all in his head because clever people do this sometimes and

he needed to see a psychiatrist. I went home and instead of going to see Paul, who was in bed very physically ill, I called his father for support and told him that I had just been to see his GP and this is what he said. His father said, 'We have been waiting for this phone call. Paul needs a psychiatrist.' I went up to the bedroom and I told Paul that he needed to see a psychiatrist and that was the worst day of my husband's life because that was the one day his GP, his own family and his wife had let him down. He was devastated. I never let him down again after that day, ever.

DC Bosomworth Would that be around February 2000?

JA Yes, I called the North Yorkshire Health Authority and told them what the GP had said, and they said that I had a right to leave the practice if I wasn't happy with the care, and that's when I went to Ripon. I asked if there were any Chronic Fatigue Syndrome-friendly doctors in the Ripon area and I found a new surgery.

DC Bosomworth Did you tell his father that you understood the significance of going down the road of psychiatry or not?

JA I can't recall whether we discussed it, but this is a problem that all of us are having with Chronic Fatigue Syndrome and it's in the government White Paper that was issued in April or May 2002.

DC Bosomworth I appreciate that, Jill, but the point is did you really agree with the psychiatric route with his father in your phone conversation?

JA   I was reserving judgement because I wanted to talk to Paul. His father was so adamant with me, I possibly agreed.

DC Bosomworth You regret agreeing.

JA   Yes. And that's when Paul said, no, I have a physical illness.

DC Bosomworth OK. Are you aware of a phone conversation between Paul and his father on the 3rd March, the year 2000, shortly after that telephone conversation where he phoned his father?

JA   And he got aggressive words from his father.

DC Bosomworth According to his father, Paul said that when you came off the phone to his father, you said, 'That was a bloody waste of time,' and that indeed you hadn't agreed with the GP regarding psychiatry. Is his father right in that or not?

JA   I can't verify that or not. I can't recall the exact conversation. I made the phone call to his father. His father agreed with the GP in Pateley Bridge. I said I had to think about this and I'd go and discuss it with Paul. And I said to Paul, 'You need a psychiatrist because this is what they're telling me you need.' I was only beginning to understand Chronic Fatigue Syndrome.

DC Bosomworth Right. Did you tell Paul the content of that conversation with the GP and also the conversation you had with his father.

JA   Yes.

DC Bosomworth　And was this the start of the family rift then or not?

JA　　　　　　　The rift had already started. It really started at his mother's funeral.

DC Bosomworth　I believe that the phone call between Paul and his father didn't go down very well with his father and the rest of the family. Am I right in thinking that his brother threatened to knock Paul's block off?

JA　　　　　　　His brother called and it was a difficult conversation.

DC Bosomworth　So it was more than threatening to knock his block off then?

JA　　　　　　　Yes.

DC Bosomworth　And did Paul threaten to go to the police?

JA　　　　　　　Paul called him back and said that we'd kept a tape of it and that he would go to the police because it actually is considered quite serious if a relative says they're going to kill you.

DC Bosomworth　Right, and regarding the phone?

Solicitor　　　　Sorry, when was that?

DC Bosomworth　It was shortly after the phone call on the 3rd of March 2000. Paul and his father obviously fell out on the phone.

JA　　　　　　　Yes.

DC Bosomworth　And did that make Paul ill?

JA　　　　　　　No, he was already physically ill.

DC Bosomworth　Well, did it make him worse?

JA　　　　　　　No.

DC Bosomworth　Right. Do you remember leaving a message on his father's answering machine saying that he had made Paul really ill?

JA	I've written that message down. You have it. It's in a red book and it never said that. It says that I'm ashamed to be associated with them because Paul has a serious physical illness.
DC Bosomworth	Why would you write it down?
JA	Because it was very important to me and it told the truth.
DC Bosomworth	OK. What do you mean by the term, 'Paul, son of Isla'? I think it's an unusual term to use.
JA	Paul was Isla's son. It was such a wonderful relationship. I felt the family were letting her down.
DC Bosomworth	Right, and was he not his father's son as well?
JA	Well of course he was.
DC Bosomworth	Right.
JA	It was just to illustrate to them that, when his mother was alive, she spent most of the time keeping the family together.
DC Bosomworth	Right. Did you want Paul to be in contact with his relatives?
JA	It's all I ever wanted and we were hoping they would say sorry for their behaviour towards us. We defended ourselves. He had a physical illness that they would not recognize. We tried to placate, negotiate and compromise with them constantly.
DC Bosomworth	Your telephone at home, has it got an answering machine?
JA	Yes.

DC Bosomworth   And is it often on the answering machine?

JA   Yes.

DC Bosomworth   Is it even on when you're at home?

JA   Yes.

DC Bosomworth   And do you let people leave messages and see who it is before you answer it?

JA   Sometimes.

DC Bosomworth   I suppose in some ways to vet calls?

JA   Not so much vet calls. I was just so busy all the time.

DC Bosomworth   If there were any messages on the machine for Paul from the family, would he have received those messages?

JA   Yes, he would. I'd never ever have prevented him from having contact with his family.

DC Bosomworth   His father's impression is that you kept the family away from Paul and didn't pass on messages.

JA   Not at all. Paul knew absolutely everything that ever happened. There were no secrets between me and Paul whatsoever, and I would never prevent him from having contact with his family. He was my husband and I joined forces with my husband. I wasn't going to let him stand there alone and be attacked by them, that's four against one.

DC Bosomworth   Right.

JA   And I wasn't prepared to let that happen to him.

May 1993

I was making watercress soup. I fried onions and garlic in a pan then poured vegetable stock over them. I took two bunches of watercress and added them to the mix. I poured the soup into bowls and mixed in fresh double cream.

'Iron. Good for you,' I said as I placed a bowl in front of each of them. They took sips and I watched their faces intently.

'Any good?'

'Mmmm,' they both said.

We had arrived on Friday evening at my godmother's house in Chichester. It was an end terrace in a 1970s block of three. She had endured a variety of troubles in her life and now lived in a home purchased for her by her brother which would go to her three nieces on her death. Her life showed in her face: it was a patchwork of worry and anxiety lines. Yet she remained stoical, entertaining and enthusiastic, and had taken to sailing with a male friend, Jim, and his sheepdog, Ben. We had walked around Chichester all day, taking in lunch at the yacht club. And then we sat by the water on the Chichester Estuary and watched clouds.

It was nippy; a chill wind blew from the ocean, making our faces raw. Seagulls seemed to hang in the air above us, screeching and calling. We huddled together, wishing for the summer. Paul and I held hands. My godmother sat slightly apart from us as we gazed up at the clouds racing across the sky. I remembered my friend Patrizia, a Colombian living in New York, and how when she visited England she had remarked on all the clouds, so many of them, so many designs, shapes and sizes, shades of greys, whites, blacks. Wispy pebbles, spirals of trailing smoke, fluffed-out cotton wool, windblown sand, an atom bomb explosion, traces of snow and fog drifting by or sailing, plumes of feathers. Many days in England were cloudy but always different, no cloud the same, yet always above us, always silent, holding rain, containing snow. The darkening skies, the charcoal black clouds of thunder.

We sat there for a long time until the tips of our fingers and toes were icy. We stood up and still the clouds raced above us. Our faces were flushed with the wind. An oystercatcher, a black and white clumsy bird, was picking at something on the mud flats. It flew off towards the clouds.

The watercress soup warmed us.

Tape 4: 25 January 2004: 11.17–11.59 continued

DC Bosomworth	So did you keep them away from him?
JA	No, I didn't. All I wanted was contact for him with them. We just waited for them either to send us a letter or make a call apologizing for their behaviour. They never did. So he told me that he wanted nothing further to do with them no matter what happened and I agreed with him.
DC Bosomworth	You say that they never wrote.
JA	I'm sorry. Yes, they did write in March of this year. His sister wrote us a letter and we both read it.
Solicitor	Last year, I think.
JA	Yes, we both read the letter. It didn't say sorry, or it might have said sorry. It said, 'We hope you're well,' but it did not acknowledge his physical illness. Granted, they couldn't see how seriously ill he'd become.

DC Bosomworth	Did you reply to that letter?
JA	No, we did not. At the end of the letter, his sister said if she did not hear from us she would leave us in peace.
DC Bosomworth	Right.
JA	Paul and I looked at each other and we said, yes. We'd prefer to be left in peace and not be involved in anymore petty arguments. Paul said, 'I am physically ill; I cannot do petty arguments with my family about torn-up birthday cards that never happened.'
DC Bosomworth	I have a copy of a letter and the original letter is actually exhibited. I think it's ALG8/1. I've also got a photocopy of the envelope, if you could read that out for me.
JA	Mr P. Anderson.
DC Bosomworth	OK and it's date stamped the 17th of March 2003. Can you just tell me if this is the letter to which you are referring, please?
JA	Yes, it is.
DC Bosomworth	Yeah and that's from his sister?
JA	Yes.
DC Bosomworth	And I think she does actually say in the letter that Paul's loved very much by the family. I think you're also right in saying that if he didn't reply to this she would leave you in peace.
JA	Yes.
DC Bosomworth	That's the last paragraph.
JA	Yes.

DC Bosomworth   But the gist of this letter, as far as I can work out, is that she's trying to build a bridge between, if you like, your side, Paul, and his father and the rest of the family. Would you agree with my interpretation of that letter and that at least his sister has gone some way, if you like, to build that bridge or attempted to build that bridge?

JA   Fair enough.

DC Bosomworth   And while I accept that maybe she hasn't said that Paul's illness is physical, she has made some attempt to heal the rift, but you and Paul haven't reciprocated, have you?

JA   No. We decided we wanted to be left in peace.

Equally important is our next heading: 'Indications of a settled intention to die'. What were the signs there which confirm that he got that set of intentions and for Jill, his wife, to see?

He had been seen by two consultant psychiatrists after his suicide bid who had found no psychiatric condition to the extent that they allowed him to go home.

It is not his first attempt. It is getting worse and worse and we know the pain is getting no better.

He must have known the distress he was causing his wife each time. He is putting her through it. He loves her; she loves him. And you know the loyalty and trust between these two people. So surely — you may conclude — this indicates part of the pattern of settled intention to die.

From the Defence's closing speech

Tape 4: 25 January 2004: 11.17–11.59 continued

DC Bosomworth What did it actually mean to you as regards things like running the household, the business?

JA I did everything. He gave me business advice, support, constant encouragement from bed. He was a wonderful husband. He would tape video programmes that I'd mentioned I wanted to watch, leave me chocolates on my pillow, just wonderful things every day.

DC Bosomworth Do you speak languages yourself?

JA No, I don't, I'm an administrator. I did the marketing and all the liaison between the clients and the translators. I hired translators to do his job.

DC Bosomworth To do Paul's job.

JA Yes.

DC Bosomworth Right.

JA His Chronic Fatigue Syndrome completely broke our hearts and shattered our lives completely, utterly and totally.

DC Bosomworth Is it fair to say, then, that you were in control of the household?

JA Yes, but we made every decision together. The only decision we never made together was his suicide. It was the last thing I ever wanted to happen to him.

DC Bosomworth What decisions did Paul make for himself, then?

JA He made all his own independent decisions

or we made every decision together. I don't really understand the question at all. Do you mean if he was free to go out and about? All he wanted to do was get out of bed and get out and about, it's all he wanted.

DC Bosomworth Did you collect his medication for him?

JA Yes. I had to because he couldn't physically get to the surgery anymore.

DC Bosomworth And did you consult directly with his doctor then?

JA Yes, I did.

DC Bosomworth Did you, at any time, make the decision yourself, if you like, to protect Paul from his family, to keep the family away from Paul?

JA No.

DC Bosomworth Because of the upset?

JA There was only one occasion when his father called to say they wanted to come and visit. I would love them to come and visit. In no way would I ever prevent contact between Paul and his family.

DC Bosomworth And would you have considered doing that?

JA Yes, I would, but with the rift.

DC Bosomworth And is that what stopped you?

JA Well, there wasn't really anything they could do.

DC Bosomworth Well, for example, they could do things like have Paul to stay for a few days or a week in order to give you a break.

JA But he wasn't well enough to travel. He

	couldn't get there. He was going by ambulances.
DC Bosomworth	Or they could have come down to your house and, for want of a better word, sat with him while you had a break yourself.
JA	But the rift had happened. We had broken off with them so there wasn't any point in asking them.
DC Bosomworth	The night you came home from Pateley Bridge, sorry, from Safeway's, you set off to Pateley and came back, then you went to Safeway's, didn't you?
JA	Yes.
DC Bosomworth	That's the night Paul took tablets.
JA	Yes.
DC Bosomworth	In many ways you controlled what happened to Paul after that, didn't you? Whether the services were found, or whether he merely slept it off, or whether he actually died that night?
JA	I went numb. I was in immediate shock.
DC Bosomworth	Do you think you had the right to make that decision?
JA	No.
DC Richardson	John's just spoken there about your relationship with Isla, Paul's mother.
JA	Yes.
DC Richardson	And was it a good one?
JA	Yes.
DC Richardson	What sort of contact did you have with her to develop this relationship?
JA	Mainly telephone contact and we talked with

	her a lot. At Rose Cottage he was well enough to have conversations with his family every week. I did talk to them and it was a wonderful relationship. We wrote letters to each other.
DC Richardson	Isla died in 1999.
JA	Yes.
DC Richardson	How long had you known her to develop this relationship?
JA	I met Paul in 1992.
DC Richardson	And you knew her from there?
JA	Yes.
DC Richardson	So how many times over these years did you meet her face to face?
JA	Probably about once a year.
DC Richardson	Did Paul ever express his concerns about his wishes if he'd died?
JA	No. I think it's just all general conversation. I mean this is a very difficult question to answer because obviously he had made two suicide attempts. As I said, my life was dedicated to saving his life so we never really discussed suicide.

There was no will.

In the case of people who do decide rationally and competently and with a settled and determined intention to commit suicide, the things that people who are suffering from these terminal illnesses, who want to die with dignity, do — you may think — is to put their affairs in order and speak to their loved ones.

None of that here.

From the Prosecution's closing speech

Tape 4: 25 January 2004: 11.17–11.59 continued

DC Richardson	Did he make any kind of will?
JA	No, he was only forty-three. We didn't get around to making wills.
DC Richardson	Right, obviously he expressed what he wished to happen after he died. Was it written anywhere?
JA	No. It was all verbal.
DC Richardson	It was obviously important to him, what happened after he died.
JA	Yes, because it's important to me.
DC Richardson	Did you discuss what you wanted to happen to you?
JA	It wasn't a big part of the conversation.
DC Richardson	Would you say that Paul's family was anything different to any other family?
JA	I don't know how I could answer that because all families seem to have disputes and fall-outs and disagreements.
DC Richardson	Would you describe them as loving?
JA	Looking back now our problem was Chronic Fatigue Syndrome. Without that we'd still have a relationship with them.
DC Bosomworth	I think it's fair to say that every member of the family that I've spoken to say they love Paul dearly.
DC Richardson	You had an opinion, along with Paul?
JA	Yes.
DC Richardson	And that family had another opinion?
JA	Yes.

DC Richardson	And that appears to have caused a major rift?
JA	Yes.
DC Richardson	They obviously visited when Paul had this disease?
JA	Yes, but he wasn't as ill then.
DC Richardson	Is it fair to say then that you resented the family's interference with the way you were dealing with Paul's illness?
JA	No, I was open to suggestions. It was the fact that they didn't believe him and that they thought he was mentally ill, not physically ill.
DC Richardson	And why did you disagree so much with that?
JA	Because he wasn't mentally ill, he was physically ill.
DC Richardson	What made you think that?
JA	I witnessed his physical state of health every day.

July 2001

It was a summer evening like many others. Lacewings fluttered through our bedroom, delicately whirling about. I had watched an orange, deep pink sunset. Now I came to him and lay beside him. He had waited, patiently. He had a mole on his neck the size of half a five-pence coin. I massaged him and, as always, he asked me to avoid it with my nails. If I scratched him, it felt like being scalded. He felt the heat of my hands on his neck. I used circular motions, left to right, right to left, up and down, semi-circle, circle, across and back. His shoulders were narrow; his slight build meant that he weighed only about nine and a half stone. He teased me about weighing less than me, and he was not much taller.

Our bodies slid into each other as we lay side by side and I soothed him. He moaned softly. Then he rolled over to face me. I massaged his sticky forehead. Fever was part of his illness and he sweated lightly, as if his body was trying to reject the poison in it. It was like malaria. My grandfather – whom everyone called 'Ga Ga', because as a child I couldn't pronounce Grandad and it stuck – had come back from Africa during the First World War with malaria. It never left him, but it was mild. This was a different disease, a different fever. He lay still as I massaged his whole body. It was a time of the evening, somewhere from 6.30 to 7, when I had finished the work that he directed and we could spend time together.

He found a music station on the radio and late into the night, while the lacewings hung from the ceiling asleep, we twirled our feet under the duvet in unison, then we hummed the theme music from *Hawaii Five-0*. He moved between stations most of the night. He had made me an earpiece connected to his radio so that if I woke up I could find out where he was. Usually he was somewhere on the other side of the world, listening to chat shows.

Tape 4: 25 January 2004: 11.17–11.59 continued

DC Richardson	I'm not going to go into the medical side of it, you've researched it a lot more than me, but couldn't this have all been in his mind?
JA	No, not at all, he'd got a virus, he was physically ill. You cannot make up Irritable Bowel Syndrome and go to the toilet fifteen times a day.

DC Richardson	Just put me right, is Irritable Bowel Syndrome separate from Chronic Fatigue Syndrome?
JA	No, Chronic Fatigue Syndrome has a catalogue of catastrophic symptoms and Irritable Bowel Syndrome is one of them.
DC Richardson	His family obviously disagreed that Paul and yourself were happy living where you were.
JA	Yes, very happy.
DC Richardson	Why was it then such an issue for his family to believe yourself and Paul?
JA	Because I think anyone with Chronic Fatigue Syndrome wants to be believed by their families and have support and comfort.
DC Richardson	So was it almost dependent on receiving some kind of confirmation?
JA	Yes.
DC Richardson	That Paul was ill?
JA	I think that's the crux of it, yes. If we could have had a bit of kindness and support from them it would have made an enormous difference to both of us.
DC Richardson	Who would have made the decision then, that that was enough to resume a relationship with the family?
JA	Paul, he made the decisions about his family. I never did, they were his family.
DC Richardson	Did you have similar problems with your family?
JA	Yes, everyone was having the same problems. You only have to call the ME Association Listening Ear and they've heard it all before.

DC Richardson	What about other people?
JA	There wasn't really anyone else. Our neighbours, Sarah and John, gave us massive support. I was getting support from the ME Association, Carers' Resource and our friends. Every day we were getting wonderful emails and gifts from them.
DC Richardson	Your neighbours Sarah and John?
JA	Yes.
DC Richardson	How were they aware of Paul's illness?
JA	I told them. John had had a kidney transplant. They were fantastic neighbours. They said, 'We're here if you want us, just knock,' and that was it.
DC Richardson	What was your reason for telling them?
JA	It's courtesy so they would know why he was in bed all the time.
DC Richardson	OK.
JA	Everyone wanted to know so I told them and I told the truth.
DC Richardson	I'm assuming that before you got in touch with his [last] doctor you also had problems with the medical profession?
JA	Yes.
DC Richardson	Was that from GPs or specialists and why did you have problems with them?
JA	It's very difficult for them. They're presented with an illness for which there is no test and no cure. How do you diagnose it? Everyone else is having the same problems.
DC Richardson	Right, OK, so what problems did you have with the medical profession?

JA	Again, not being believed and Paul asking for medication and them saying to him that he didn't need it. There was nothing wrong.
DC Richardson	Did the doctors then, having not believed you, mention psychological problems instead?
JA	Yes.
DC Richardson	How did Paul react to that?
JA	It was difficult for us because when you're very physically ill, and you know you're not making it up mentally, you'd like some support. All they have to say is this is a serious physical illness, we can't cure you and then suggest some kind of medication for a person to try. Well they didn't.
DC Richardson	Wasn't Paul prescribed?
JA	Paul asked for medication and we told them that we knew they didn't understand this disease. We don't expect a cure but can he try this, and that was our approach to the medical profession.
DC Richardson	Is it right to say then that the doctors disagreed with your opinion?
JA	Yes. We wanted support for a physical illness. We wanted a GP to suggest this illness exists.
DC Richardson	And you carried on until you eventually settled with his last GP?
JA	Yes.
DC Richardson	Who, I think, you described as CFS-friendly?
JA	Yes. And this is standard Chronic Fatigue Syndrome. There was an ME support group in Harrogate. They sent three adults to

Harrogate District Hospital to talk to consultants about ME. They had a discussion
about how Chronic Fatigue Syndrome or ME
was affecting them and their relatives. There
were three adults in their fifties and they all
cried when they came out to the car park
because of the consultants' response to them.

DC Richardson   How was his doctor able to do things or what
was he able to do that the other doctors, who
didn't quite believe you or didn't believe you
at all, weren't able to do?

JA   He gave Paul a bit of kindness. He issued
medication and listened to him. He's considered the best doctor in Ripon. He has a
fantastic reputation.

DC Bosomworth   You made the decision after his death not to
contact his family?

JA   Yes, because that was his decision.

DC Bosomworth   And the same regarding the funeral?

JA   Yes, he said under no circumstances are you
ever to have any contact with my family. I
thought about it morally and took advice
from friends. I decided to write the letter to
his cousin, Russell Brown, who had kept in
contact by sending just one Christmas card.

Tape 5: 25 January 2004: 12.00–12.44

DC Bosomworth   We were just talking about his eldest sister
and it is her opinion that Paul died unneces-
sarily because if you, Jill, had found looking
after him difficult, the door was always open

	and anyone within the family would have helped. Did you ever ask for help?
JA	They didn't accept that he was physically ill and they all had their own lives. We were in Yorkshire. I had immense support from other people.
DC Bosomworth	So did you ever ask the family for help?
JA	Probably not, I don't recall.
DC Bosomworth	When was Paul's funeral?
JA	I can't remember the date. It was in Harrogate.
DC Bosomworth	Can you remember the month?
JA	I'm sorry, I can't recall because I was in deep grief. I'm going to do a life ceremony for him in the future and there will be lots of friends and family attending who gave us massive support throughout his illness.
DC Bosomworth	Right. Paul's family were not informed?
JA	I thought about it carefully. He had asked, said to me if anything ever happened to him I was never to have any further contact with them whatsoever.
DC Bosomworth	So, is that why they weren't informed of his death?
JA	Initially, and then I talked to friends and my family and I decided because his cousin Russell had sent us a Christmas card over the years that I would contact him. Paul was incredibly grateful for Russell. Paul said at least Russell can see there's another side to this story. Paul's family were antagonistic, we couldn't fight with them.

DC Bosomworth	You believed Russell could see another side?
JA	Yes.
DC Bosomworth	And I believe you actually contacted Russell, didn't you?
JA	Yes, I did. I sent him a letter.
DC Bosomworth	I have a copy of that letter. I haven't got the original. Obviously that's with Russell Brown, but I have exhibited the copy as MAW1 and I think that came from his younger sister. I'd just like you to confirm for me if that's the letter you sent to Russell please?
JA	Yes, it is.
DC Bosomworth	I think that is your signature.
Solicitor	Could I have a look at that, please? Thank you.
DC Bosomworth	I think you included this with it, is that right?
JA	Yes, that's my tribute to Paul.
DC Bosomworth	Yeah, but that was originally addressed to Hal.
JA	And Yasue.
DC Bosomworth	Yasue, but I think you've sent this to a fair few people, haven't you?
JA	Yes I have, our friends.
DC Bosomworth	That's your tribute to him, isn't it?
JA	Yes, it is.
DC Bosomworth	When did you actually send the letter to Russell?
JA	I think it was around early January.
DC Bosomworth	I'm assuming you didn't want them at the funeral?
JA	No, I preferred them not to come. The

funeral was very simple, because of everything's that happened and this situation I'm in today. I just had him cremated in Harrogate. That's what he wanted. My brother and sister-in-law came with me.

DC Bosomworth And where are his ashes now?

JA They're with me.

DC Bosomworth So at the moment then there's no grave site, if you like, or headstone?

JA No, he didn't want that. He wanted his ashes to be scattered.

DC Bosomworth And is that what you propose to do?

JA Yes.

DC Bosomworth The middle paragraph of this letter to Russell says, 'At his express wishes,' and his being Paul, 'at his express wishes and also mine I wish no further contact with his remaining family.'

JA Yes.

DC Bosomworth 'Out of respect for Isla I cannot contact, I cannot go further in this statement.'

JA Yes.

DC Bosomworth When did Paul express that to you?

JA After he tried to attempt to talk to his father three or four times on the telephone. I was with Paul in the room. I didn't hear all of the conversation but Paul was very gentle and kind, trying to persuade his father to listen to him, that he had a serious physical illness and a virus. His father was being difficult with him and then that's really when Paul decided that.

DC Bosomworth	And was it mentioned prior to, immediately prior to, his last suicide attempt?
JA	No, it might have been.
DC Bosomworth	Did he mention it after the suicide attempt when you came home?
JA	Possibly, I don't know, we didn't talk about them a lot. We tried; we were deeply, deeply hurt by their behaviour towards us. We couldn't understand it.
DC Bosomworth	Didn't you expect Russell Brown to contact the family?
JA	Yes, I did. I wanted them to know.
DC Bosomworth	So couldn't you have done this sooner through Russell Brown?
JA	I could, but with everything that's happened I was in deep grief and, originally, I wasn't ever going to tell them, but other people persuaded me to change my mind, which was the moral thing to do.
DC Bosomworth	Don't you think they had a moral right to grieve for Paul?
JA	Yes.
DC Bosomworth	Do you think Paul would have actually wanted them to attend his funeral?
JA	No, absolutely not.
DC Bosomworth	His sister says, or feels, you took total control of Paul, particularly after Isla had died when he was vulnerable.
JA	No.
DC Bosomworth	Other members of the family have intimated the same thing. Do you think they're right?

JA   No. Paul was his own man. He was his own
            master. You can go and see the Head of the
            Rheumatology Department at Harrogate
            District Hospital. He will tell you.

February 2003

The ambulance crew arrived at Westowe Cottage on the lane
with no name. We were going to see the Head of Rheumatology
at the local hospital. Paul had insisted that this consultant should
see him and he got his GP to issue letters. Paul was adamant that
he had inflammation, even though all the blood tests had come
back normal. I had worked late into the night for a client and I
was stretched. It was the first time Paul had gone for a hospital
appointment wearing his pyjamas. He did not really need clothes
anymore.

It was a rustling, breezy February day. Everything outside
looked soggy, as if it had snowed and thawed. Yet the air was
fresh and raw. The two-man crew hauled him into the ambulance
with soft encouraging words, and deposited him on the narrow
bed inside. They were agreeable and easy, their talk light and
rhythmic. I sat back and enjoyed the lull. Paul and I were both
glassy-eyed with lack of sleep. He curled up and braced himself.
The crew tried to banter with us, but we were moody and bleak.
They exchanged glances and let us be.

Paul felt every bump and crevice in the road as the vehicle
made its way. We passed through the village where we had lived
in Rose Cottage. The cottage stood silent at the centre; nothing
stirred. Smoke drifted from some of the chimneys and I worked
out who was in and who was out, even though there was no
point, nothing had changed.

When we reached the hospital, the crew found a wheelchair

for him and placed him in it. They briskly manoeuvred him through the main entrance, past the reception desk and turned left to a bank of lifts. The Rheumatology Department was on the second floor. The hospital seemed endless and subterranean, cream or brown corridors sprawled in all directions. We passed wards where people attached to drips blinked back at us. We finally reached the department and the crew wheeled him into a private consultation room and lifted him carefully onto a hospital bed. They exchanged looks again. We waited; we were twenty minutes early. Paul was shattered already, his face ghostly, and it was only 11.30 a.m. I needed coffee: he waved me away and reluctantly I left him.

When I returned, the consultant had arrived and already begun his examination. He had sandy brown hair close cropped to his skull and deep-set eyes. His manner was efficient. He was lifting Paul's arm, to be greeted by a yelp.

'Your cartilage has calcified,' he stated.

Paul and I exchanged looks; it was sudden shock. As if we did not know already, but we did not want to hear the truth. A far-away look entered Paul's eyes and it never left him again.

Paul raised himself up somehow and said, 'I'm fighting for my survival.' Then he went through a concise description of the symptoms of ME/CFS. The consultant listened. It was obvious that there was nothing he could do for Paul.

'Where did you get the idea for Remicade/infliximab and the thalidomide drug?' the consultant asked.

Paul gave an academic response. The consultant listened, his eyes narrowed. Paul sank back.

'You can go for another blood test,' the consultant said. He scribbled something and shoved the paperwork into my hands, then scuttled off.

We did not have to look at each other. I helped Paul back into the wheelchair and steered him out of the room. The consultant was standing in another office with the door open, talking to a woman. Paul's hair was all over the place and ruffled at the back of his neck. I tried to go carefully and as quickly as possible. His mood was hostile. He gripped the arms of the wheelchair and somehow we reached the blood department. A nurse took his blood. We barely exchanged words.

Later we waited in the cold for the ambulance crew to collect us. He sat in his wheelchair outside the hospital that he had visited and stayed in for so many years. And now he was leaving it virtually immobile. I lit a cigarette for him and placed it in his mouth. He had started smoking again this year. I had yelled and screamed at him, but he was dying so it did not make much difference. He sucked on it. He looked at me as if he was swimming into even murkier water, a whirlpool taking him down rapidly, a long sinking and a slow drowning. The anger drifted out of us; we said nothing to each other.

The same two-man crew returned and put him back in the ambulance. There was an elderly woman with us on the journey. She sat on the seat behind the driver's and we listened as she told us about her considerable health problems. By the time we reached her home in Ripon, we had a concise knowledge of her entire life history. The crew checked she had a family member or friend coming soon, then lifted her into her home. We started the journey back to Westowe Cottage. Paul lay prone and desperate and closed his eyes. The ambulance drifted past slushy fields as the crew negotiated the lanes and I gave them directions. One of the men talked about how he had taken the paramedic exam eight times and failed. Paul responded, 'Don't give up, you'll pass.'

We got home. The ambulance crew helped him to the door then I took over. We reached the lounge. He shook me off. He walked to the fireplace, shoulders stooped and frail. I couldn't do anything. He stood a moment and then made his way upstairs. Later I smashed the irons into the fire, over and over again. He screamed at me from above, to stop making so much noise.

She had saved his life three times and you may conclude she must have realized she could not go on forever, watching every moment, praying he would remain alive.

All the things she did for him. She did everything that he wanted and felt necessary for his medication, for his treatment, for his welfare. She respected his intellect and judgement and, more importantly, she loved him devotedly.

'I should have called the ambulance. He would have been alive.' That was her wish now, and if I may say, it is the only selfish thing — perhaps — she has ever said in respect of her husband.

From the Defence's closing speech

Tape 5: 25 January 2004: 12.00–12.44 continued

DC Bosomworth	What was your relationship with Isla?
JA	It was the most fantastic. I couldn't have had a better mother-in-law. I couldn't believe my luck. It was a wonderful relationship.
DC Bosomworth	And was that all the way through to her death?
JA	Yes, it was getting better.
DC Richardson	What sort of contact did you have with her to develop this relationship?
JA	Mainly telephone and we talked with them a lot. He was well enough at Rose Cottage to

have conversations with them every week
and I did talk to them. It was a wonderful
relationship. We picked seeds from our
garden at Rose Cottage and sent them as gifts
to them.

August 1998

We sat on our throne chairs, which were high-backed, green and
made of plastic. They came from a DIY store, B&Q. We surveyed our kingdom. The kingdom that we had made together –
a garden at the back of Rose Cottage. We had moved there from
Pateley Bridge in the Christmas of 1996. Two years and seven
months later, we could survey the results of our collaboration,
mostly my labour and his design, and we had our slice of Eden.
He sank back into the chair, closed his eyes and reached for my
hand. I gave it willingly and we relaxed.

The fullness of the harvest we were reaping was all around
us. Bees lingered among the sweetpeas that threaded up canes.
Butterflies, dusky red admirals and bright eye-spotted peacocks,
clustered around the buddleia bushes that he had grown from
seed. An easy plant, happy anywhere, and often seen blooming
beside railway lines. The butterflies suckled on the purple, pink
and white spires of the flowers. The pond that he had made was
home to a town of creepy crawlies that went about their business
with as much assurance as any city slicker. Skaters criss-crossed
the surface, frogs sprawled among the stones at the edges, and
snails sucked the bottom. A small, tiny scratch in the planet's
surface – yet how this pond yielded life. I thought of the William
Blake poem: 'To see a world in a grain of sand, And a heaven in
a wild flower, Hold infinity in the palm of your hand, And eter-
nity in an hour.'

The garden had been a rubbish tip at the beginning. I had filtered the clay soil for stones and refuse. And then I had mixed in compost. A local farmer had given us a tractor-load of manure. Now the soil was rich as black liquorice. Paul had made the lawns, all three of them, interspersed with beds of wild flowers and perennials. The lawns were flat as pancakes and, as we surveyed them, shone like bowling greens. Here we were, king and queen of this patch, just like everyone else who makes a garden in England. This small country where land is premium and gardening is second nature.

The garden was a long strip of land, varying in width. On one side it was bordered by a high sheltering hedge, beyond which were farmers' fields. Down the other side, a wooden fence divided us from our neighbours. And into this piece of land we had poured seeds of all varieties purchased from catalogues. We had read gardening books and magazines in bed late at night and cut out the sections that interested us. When there was a howling gale outside we potted up on the lounge floor, spreading newspaper to protect the carpet. He had his seeds and I had mine. I had bought brown paper packets and stickers with flowers on them, and I collected and dried seeds for our families.

The vegetable patch was the first section of the garden. It was filled with potatoes. We grew first early, second early and main crop. August, and underground the main crop was pumping juice into the large spuds. The red and white flowers of runner beans twirled around canes and, on inspection, the buds were beginning to grow into pods. The harvest was coming in. Earlier in the season, peas had curled up a fence of twigs collected from a local wood. Sweetcorn stood in a regiment of diagonal lines, beginning to ripen. Strawberries rambled among the rows. Spinach, lettuce and carrots streaked through a bed

interwoven with red, gold and orange marigolds and Cali-
fornian poppies. The light green foliage of parsnips reached to
knee height, leaving the fruit of the roots below only to the
imagination. The burgundy-stalked leaves of succulent chard
and juicy beetroot mingled together. Groups of sunflowers
towered over the patch, lifting their golden heads to the warmth
and light.

There was a loud cry and a snuffling at the bottom of the
garden. A net around a patch of strawberries started to shake
furiously. We got up in unison. Something was trapped; something was crying. When we reached the bed we saw that a
hedgehog had got itself tangled up. It was rolled up into a tight
ball. He delicately caught hold of the hedgehog and gently
stretched out its body, unwinding the net and loosening its claws
from where they had got caught. The creature was prone and
looked dead. It hardly moved. I looked at him for advice. He told
me to fetch water and bread. I returned with a bowl. He placed
it in front of the creature, which lay motionless on the ground.
He said, 'Give it some time, it'll recover.' When we returned
some hours later to the spot where it had lain, the hedgehog had
gone.

Later, we sat in the lounge and he worked on a piece of wood.
He had found a branch in a glade that he chiselled, sculpted and
hewed. It was to be a walking stick. When it was finished, my
mother used it for a while before bringing it back to me. I plan
to use it later, much later, when my body is slow. I plan to lean
on it and roll it in my gnarled fist if I get old. When we finally
clambered into bed, the heat clung to us. We thought of the
hedgehog.

A letter came the next day nominating us for Best Translation
Company in Britain. Here was more satisfaction than anything
else we could think of. We shared it between us all day. We called

his family and my family with our good news. His mother said to us, 'I always knew you could do it.' She was always there at the end of the telephone with her kindness and approval.

Whatever views he had about not liking psychiatrists, we say – without question – he was a man of sound mind; of some intellect. If they have determined to die then unless you put them in a straitjacket and force-feed them, how do you prevent someone who has made up his mind to die from taking his own life?

For Paul Anderson had normal life expectancy; he was forty-three. He had another thirty–forty years of what you may think he saw as unremitting pain . . . and he has the right to choose to die.

From the Defence's closing speech

Tape 5: 25 January 2004: 12.00–12.44 continued

DC Richardson	So about this relationship. Obviously Isla died in 1999.
JA	Yes.
DC Richardson	This issue about the birthday card that was torn up or thrown away, was petty.
JA	Yes.
DC Richardson	And that you treasured the things that Isla sent.
JA	Yes.
DC Richardson	Like that birthday card.
JA	Yes.
DC Richardson	Where are those birthday cards now?
JA	It's a long time ago and I don't think most people keep their birthday cards, do they?

DC Richardson	Was there anything that you've kept at all relating to what Isla gave you?
JA	There were bits and pieces. Just a moment, I'll have a word with my solicitor.
DC Bosomworth	Do you want to consult him and stop the interview?
JA	No, it's OK.
Solicitor	Right, perhaps if you want to ask us another question.
DC Bosomworth	And come back to that, is that OK with you, Jill?
JA	Yes.
DC Bosomworth	Right.

March 1999

He had cried throughout the night. I could do nothing except say inane things. He did not cry often – I cried more than him – but when he did it was always a release. It was better between us, afterwards.

'She'll always be with you.'

He took no notice. 'Mam, Mam.'

We dressed in a misty dawn that turned into a bright day. The sky was cobalt blue with everything lit sharply in the sunshine and the buds getting bigger day by day. As we left Rose Cottage, our neighbours Dot and Tony came out and asked us where we were going. I told them, and we both climbed into the car. We had a red Rover. He drove the two-hour journey to Gretna. We did not speak, or if we did we made banal comments. When we crossed the bridge into this small town, we did not yell 'Scotland!' as we usually did.

We had seen her twice in the weeks beforehand. Once in

hospital and once when they sent her home to die. There was nothing else they could do. Her doctor had hugged her when he told her it was over. She had waited two days after Paul's birthday to depart on the 27th of February 1999. And now she lay in the funeral parlour.

We drove past the shopping precinct with its turf accountants, off-licence and butchers. Discarded newspapers flapped in the gutters. It all looked battered, small and mean. We drove down the streets to his sister's house. There were the usual empty, boarded-up houses, and then a council estate. It was modern and had been thoughtfully designed. The brick houses were all two storey and set in a square around a large green, but there was not much on the green, just scruffy grass where the children played and their parents and grandparents took their dogs. His sister lived next door to a rowdy family and because Paul's family were kind to them, his mother said they felt protected. She had told me all kinds of stories about them. As we arrived, I looked at their house. It was unkempt and untidy. The yard was muddy and full of rubbish. On the other hand, my sister-in-law's husband had worked hard and her house was neat and trim. Their front garden now boasted exotic trees and shrubs amid gravel. As we entered this small house, I could take in no more than that it was spotless and painted an exotic colour.

The family were all there, crammed into the lounge. His younger sister and her husband made a fuss as we entered and greeted us with hugs and kisses. Children seemed to be everywhere, nieces and nephews, and his brother and his wife, his sister and her husband. His father had changed into his best suit, and his eldest son, Paul's brother, said to him, 'Why are you wearing that?'

'Because she would want me to,' he had replied.

The clink of cups of strong tea seemed to be endless. Paul's brother-in-law had bought the house and they had embarked on a programme of redecoration every six months or so. Paul's sister showed me artwork that they had made together. Her husband was an art teacher and deputy head of a school. I told her it was good enough to sell. It was a distraction; none of us really knew what to say to each other. We all wanted the same thing: for Isla to be with us.

The funeral cars arrived. Paul and his father and siblings went in one car; the spouses in another. I tried to make small talk, but no one was in the mood and I fell silent. It took us less than five minutes to get to the church, which was a gigantic monolith of grey Scottish architecture. It seemed to loom over the community with its great spires. We sat through the service that she had meticulously planned. Paul leant over, clutching his stomach. I wished he had had some breakfast, but he had refused. His sister read a eulogy for Isla. It was filled with memories of her kindness. I looked around, from where we were sitting in the front pews. The church had high ceilings and I shivered. It was packed. It seemed that the whole community in Gretna had turned out for Isla. They all looked worn out and decent, all much older than their years. Everyone wore their best, the best that they could do. People snuffled and rose for the hymns. Paul remained seated as we all stood. The service ended with 'What a Wonderful World' by Louis Armstrong and tears rolled freely. Then Paul bent over further and looked at me.

'I'm going to be sick.'

I turned to the person who was sitting next to me. 'Do you have a plastic bag?' I said.

She just looked back at me absently. I looked at my handbag: it was tiny.

'Your hat,' he whispered.

I removed the hat. It was a gift from my brother and his girl-friend. It was a Russian affair with a black fake-fur trim. Paul was duly sick into it, quietly. I looked at my ruined hat. The congregation was leaving the church; people were drifting out as if in a trance. Paul and I staggered out. I held the hat like a bunch of flowers. I asked a few people if they knew where a bin was, but they shook their heads and walked on. I asked one of his sisters and she told me to just get rid of it. I ended up placing the hat on a bench in the church's vestibule. When I told the priest, he looked at me as if I was from another country. In silence, we stepped back into the family funeral cars. It was the same arrangement: I was with the spouses; I hated to be parted from him. No one said anything but I tried to make small talk again with one of his brothers-in-law.

'You have a wonderful singing voice,' I mumbled to him.

He had sung at the service and was in the local choir in the town where they lived. He muttered something back and looked out of the car window. I gave up and stared at the hearse, which was two cars in front of us. We reached the crematorium. It was an oblong concrete building. We sat through another service and watched as she in her coffin went through the window into the mock flames. Nothing would be the same ever again without the peacekeeper and arbiter of the family. His father was bowed in front of us. Then we all stumbled out into the sunshine and for some reason I said, 'What a beautiful day' to one of Paul's aunties. She nodded. Then I felt awful. The funeral party stood outside the crematorium blinking at each other in the light. We were in a large gravelled area where all the wreaths were stretched out in long rows for each of the departed that day. We tried to think of something to say to each other. His sisters stayed close to his father, and if I approached I felt their hostility, their protection of their father. I smiled awkwardly at them and turned to Paul. We walked around the mass of flowers and read each other messages from the relatives and friends, but we were looking for ours and found them. His younger sister had ordered them for us. Our flowers were there with the note attached that he had written for her and us:

Unseen, we feel your eyes upon us, guiding, caring, loving.
For love is love, so strong that nothing can destroy the
bonds that bind us.
We are not, and never shall be alone.
Always and Forever.
Love Paul and Jill
Xxxxxxx

His cousin Russell approached us. He was small in stature and balding, but looked efficiently clean. I had never met him before as he was always in Westminster. I did not know what to say to him so I said, 'We see you on TV sometimes.' He nodded, stared at me and then evaporated away muttering something about not being able to stay long. I never met him again. We liked Russell's mother, Auntie Muriel, and had visited her in Annan several years before. She lived in a two-up two-down and was a chain-smoker. Her daughter had got into a car one night, a lift to an event. Muriel had not wanted her to go. Her daughter did not come back. There was a horrific car crash. Muriel could not forgive herself.

We returned to the cars. I felt like saying that we should go home. Paul's face was a deep grey colour. I was worried he would pass out. I asked him if he would like to continue; he said yes. We arrived at the wake in a school hall. It was a long room with a table at one end covered with plates of sandwiches and the rest of the room set up with tables and chairs like a restaurant.

Tea flowed freely. Everyone descended on the food. We were all ravenous. His younger sister showed me a photograph of Isla in her forties, when they lived in Zimbabwe. I hardly recognized her. She looked so young and vibrant. I asked his sister if I could have a copy. She pursed her lips and changed the conversation. I turned to some of the other friends and relatives, who were all standing around, munching. Paul was slumped at the food table at the far end. I made conversation and then went to him.

The children sat with us; they were downcast and despondent. I talked to them individually and asked the usual questions, how school was going, their friends and their hobbies. They were all sweet and slowly their despondency lifted: they became animated and noisy and got up to start playing their games. Paul sat crouched, unable to make much conversation. His family sat at a large table at the far end of the hall. I did not speak to them. I could tell by the look on their faces that they were not impressed with Paul. I stood up to speak to some more of the relatives I liked, Uncle Tom and Auntie Jean, Gus and his wife. They asked me what was wrong with Paul. I told them that we really did not know. The doctors could find nothing but we both knew he was physically ill. They murmured their concern and their eyes were kind, but all our thoughts were with Isla. I sat back down and some of the younger relatives joined me. The sister of his brother-in-law and her boyfriend chatted away about other people who should have attended. Other family feuds that prevented estranged cousins and so on from being there. I looked at Paul. He sat alone and silent at the table. He was bent over, and his chin was almost on the table. I went to him.

'I think I should get you home,' I said.

He agreed. I helped him to his feet and we started to make our way out of the hall. I let a few of the relatives know we were leaving and they wished us well. A friend of one of his sisters,

Lawrence, said he would send some information he had about ME/CFS. I said we did not think it was that. Paul had been diagnosed with post-viral disability. I gave him our address. Paul said, 'I'm sorry, I'm not well, we have to go.' Then we walked past the table where his family sat and walked on. His father and younger sister got up and followed us. They came out onto the street and I apologized to them.

'We have to go,' I said. 'We wish we could stay, sorry.'

They said to me, 'We just want you to be happy.'

I said, 'We are.'

Paul turned to his dad and said, 'Sorry, Dad.' Then we left.

The journey home was tedious. Paul insisted on driving. He said it would help him forget the pain. I sat back and thought, What an awful day, what a truly awful day. How could we cope without Isla and her kindness and her support? How would we get through each moment without her? I knew Paul was thinking the same thing.

Tape 5: 25 January 2004: 12.00–12.44 continued

DC Richardson	You obviously discussed Paul's wishes in respect of his ashes being scattered. What other things did you discuss regarding what should happen after his death?
JA	We both told each other what we wanted to happen to us if we died. We both wanted to be cremated and have our ashes scattered.
DC Richardson	I think that was going to be my second question really. Was there any specific reason that he was discussing events after his death with you?

JA	We were just like any other couple who discuss those things because they are important.
DC Richardson	You mentioned he expressed his wishes constantly.
JA	It wasn't constantly, no.
DC Richardson	I have a relationship with my wife. I suppose I have discussed what I'd like to happen after my death but I certainly don't do it constantly unless I suppose there was a fear that I was going to die. Did Paul ever express those concerns?
JA	No. I think it's just all general conversation.
DC Richardson	Obviously, there were previous suicide attempts as well. Do you think that was why he was expressing his wishes?
JA	He expressed them for instance when he had difficulties with his family, when he was saying, 'Please, Dad, can we sort this out? I've caught a virus.'
DC Richardson	And that family had another opinion?
JA	Yes.
DC Richardson	And that appears to have caused a major rift?
JA	Yes. He just didn't want further contact with them. It was his decision. He tried hard to negotiate with them via telephone. And told me, one of them said he wanted to kill him.
DC Richardson	That's strong words, wanting to kill somebody just because they're ill.
JA	Yes.
DC Richardson	I'm trying to work out why this would have been said.
JA	Why does anyone want to kill anyone else?

Solicitor	Do you know what the gist of the conversation was?
JA	No. The relative called and left a message on the tape machine.
DC Richardson	Were you in the room when this happened?
JA	No.
DC Richardson	Were you there when Paul was speaking to him?
JA	No, Paul went to the phone and called him back and said if you call here again I'll bite your head off.
DC Richardson	So you're not aware of the gist of the conversation that was left on the answering machine?
JA	No.
DC Richardson	So how do you know that he was abusive then?
JA	That's what Paul said.
DC Richardson	So Paul has discussed this with you?
JA	Yes.
DC Richardson	What did Paul say to you?
JA	That the relative had called and . . . had murder on his brain.
DC Richardson	And that was it.
JA	Yes.
DC Richardson	Did he mention any reason for him wanting to kill Paul?
JA	No.
DC Richardson	Did he mention because it was the way that Paul had spoken to his father?
JA	Paul was lovely to his father. I was in the room and obviously his father wouldn't

	listen to him so Paul probably lost his temper.
DC Richardson	Were you ever told by Paul that he lost his temper with his father and spoke out of line?
JA	I've been in the room with him and heard him. I mean he was just like the rest of us, just sort of lose your temper when your family won't listen to you and accept that you are physically ill.
DC Richardson	Right, because it appears from speaking to the family that Paul has had a conversation with his father on the telephone. I don't know fully what it was about but he spoke out of turn to his father, which Paul's relative found out about and was disgusted with the way Paul had spoken to his father and called him up saying if you do that I'll knock your block off. Nothing has been mentioned about killing or threats to kill. Now obviously that's some other person's side of the story, now unfortunately Paul's not here to say what happened. I'm asking if you were told by Paul what was said and how do you know that the telephone call wasn't true if you never heard it, or the other side of the conversation?
JA	Because Paul told me the truth. What was the point in lying?
DC Richardson	Right, so . . .
JA	I was in the room with lots of these other conversations going on between them. As I said, it was four against one.

DC Richardson	Right, this is what I was trying to get at earlier, you have mentioned that there was abuse, that there was this, and I'm trying to get to the gist of it. So you've mentioned there was some problem with his sister and diet.
JA	We had a conversation about that but she got very upset. She was telling me what I should be feeding Paul, but I was already feeding him organic food and vegetables, fresh not processed food, everything I could think of to get him well.
DC Richardson	Were you being contacted by other members of the family?
JA	I was just trying. You can only take so much. I was trying to be extremely pleasant to them most of the time and listen to their advice and say yes I am doing that, but I found them very difficult.
DC Richardson	What else were their problems? I can understand that they didn't agree with your and Paul's diagnosis. I can understand that because they can't see Paul, they are interested in his welfare and maybe speaking about diet but what else was their problem against Paul or Paul and yourself?
JA	I don't know – there seemed to be a lot of jealousy.
DC Richardson	In what way?
JA	My instinct was that Paul's mother loved them all equally, but she loved Paul slightly more than the rest of them and they were a bit jealous of that.

DC Richardson	Is that instinct or do you have anything that puts you in that frame of mind?
JA	I don't know how to respond to that really. Family relationships are difficult. They were extremely difficult with Paul's family. After Isla died, everything changed and it shouldn't have happened and it did.
DC Richardson	And what made you think that, because Paul said or is there anything else?
JA	No.
DC Richardson	I don't and I'm not even going to go into the medical side of it, you've researched it a lot more than me, but could this not have all been in his mind?
JA	No, not at all, he had a virus, he was physically ill. He also said that, in the future, there will be viruses like this for example in biological warfare.
DC Richardson	How did he know this then?
JA	He was a brilliant man. He listened to short-wave radio and satellite.
DC Richardson	Where was he getting this information from?
JA	I've just told you, programmes . . . and also I went on the Chronic Fatigue Syndrome website in America, which was my main source of support and information.
DC Richardson	So how?
JA	Paul suggested infliximab and I typed in infliximab/Remicade on the site and one article came up written by two professors which completely vindicated Paul.

DC Richardson	How did Paul get to know this information a few weeks before he died?
JA	I took the article in to him. I printed it off the Internet and I said, 'You have been vindicated.' This is an exact match of your medical records.
DC Richardson	Three weeks before he died he was able to read and digest information.
JA	No, he didn't read it.
DC Richardson	You just said he read it.
JA	I'm wrong. He did not read it, I told him.
DC Richardson	You told him, how did you tell him?
JA	I probably waved it in front of him and said, 'You are vindicated, isn't that fantastic news?'
DC Richardson	Did you read it out to him?
JA	Probably bits of it.
DC Richardson	I've got no further questions. Have you, John?
DC Bosomworth	It's just a couple of things you've brought up yourself actually.
JA	Yes.
DC Bosomworth	And one thing that I wasn't going to touch on medically in this interview but we have touched on it slightly. Who first diagnosed Chronic Fatigue Syndrome?
JA	As far as I recall it was a chest specialist that Paul went to see on his own at Harrogate District Hospital. I can't remember the name of this consultant. Paul came home and said he'd been diagnosed with post-viral disability.

DC Bosomworth   Right, so it wasn't something you diagnosed between yourselves off the Internet then?

JA   No.

DC Bosomworth   OK.

JA   Obviously we started doing research. Paul always said he didn't have ME. It's now becoming standard with the medical profession that they are eliminating the word ME. It hasn't happened for all the different organizations and they are going with Chronic Fatigue Syndrome.

DC Bosomworth   Basically, sorry, Jill, I'll just check again. Basically it wasn't self-diagnosis of the Chronic Fatigue Syndrome?

JA   No.

DC Bosomworth   That'll do then, no's the answer. Yeah, you said Paul made his own decisions?

JA   Yes.

DC Bosomworth   OK, is there anything you want to add at this point?

JA   We only moved to Yorkshire to be near our families and we lost Paul's family because of Chronic Fatigue Syndrome.

DC Bosomworth   Anything from your solicitor at this point?

Solicitor   No.

We are not all lawyers, thank goodness, and we do not all approach things in a legalistic fashion. People in despair do not weigh carefully the pros and cons.

He had every reason to want to die ... his pain was unremitting ... he had lost his job, gone bankrupt and, you may think, lost his self-respect. He had tried all sorts of medication. Next he had

tried every sort of doctor imaginable – immunologists, rheumatol-
ogists . . . the whole gamut – over a period of eight years. No doctor
had been able to offer him realistic hope or alleviate the constant pain.

From the Defence's closing speech

Tape 6: 25 January 2004: 13.27–14.10

DC Bosomworth	Can you just confirm that all persons here have identified themselves?
JA	Yes.
DC Bosomworth	And also that since the last interview and this interview, we haven't discussed your case with you?
JA	No.
DC Bosomworth	Right. There's a couple of things from the last interview that I'd like to raise really.
JA	Yes.
DC Bosomworth	You said, I think you said, that Paul's arms had begun to shrink.
JA	His bones were grinding in his arms and he was losing the use of his arms. It was a long, slow decline.
DC Bosomworth	Right.
JA	Since Paul died, a friend of ours, who has a similar condition, Chronic Fatigue Syndrome . . .
DC Bosomworth	Yeah.
JA	In America, it's not as bad as Paul's. She sent me an article from New Jersey via email from Imperial College London.

They had just done some clinical research where they tested thirty healthy people and thirty people who had Chronic Fatigue Syndrome and the scientists found a virus in the muscle of the people with Chronic Fatigue Syndrome. So that might explain why his bones had started to crumble, because the virus was in the muscle and his arms were getting thinner.

DC Bosomworth Yeah, right, by shrink then, did you mean thinner?

JA Yes.

DC Bosomworth Or shorter?

JA Thinner, yes.

DC Bosomworth Thinner.

JA I'd say thinner. He had thought of the thalidomide drug, which is interesting.

DC Bosomworth Say that again.

JA He had thought of the thalidomide drug. Which is interesting.

DC Bosomworth But he hadn't actually taken that drug?

JA No. I don't think they'd give him access. It would need to be clinically trialled.

DC Bosomworth OK.

JA For Chronic Fatigue Syndrome.

DC Bosomworth I believe three weeks before he died he was too ill to read?

JA He . . .

DC Bosomworth My colleague mentioned the article that you trawled off the Internet.

JA Three professors, er two professors, yes . . .

DC Bosomworth Yeah.

JA	Had written it.
DC Bosomworth	Ah, but Paul was unable to read that, why was that?
JA	He was very, very ill and he would make a decision about what he was going to read and not read and that was one of the things he didn't need to read because I was able to tell him verbally the gist of the article.
DC Bosomworth	Right. So was he . . .
JA	He didn't need to read it.
DC Bosomworth	Was he able to read it, then?
JA	He was trying to conserve his energy. Yes, of course he could read it, but he was trying to conserve his energy.
DC Bosomworth	Right, so physically he could actually read it if he wanted to?
JA	If he wanted to, yes.
DC Bosomworth	Right, so he wasn't too ill, for example, he couldn't pick the magazine up to read?
JA	He could pick magazines up to read.
DC Bosomworth	Right and his . . .
JA	He was being extremely selective at that point in time. He was very, very ill.
DC Bosomworth	And his eyesight didn't mean that he couldn't see the article?
JA	Oh, that's right, he could see it, yes.
DC Bosomworth	Right.
JA	But he didn't need to read it. I just gave him an overview, simplifying it for him.
DC Bosomworth	I mentioned in your first interview that we've been told you had a previous marriage. Did you get married?

JA   No, I did not. I was on my own for years and I waited for him.

DC Bosomworth   I'm just a little confused as to where the family's got this notion from.

JA   I've no idea.

DC Bosomworth   Because they're saying they got it from Paul.

JA   I've no idea. Paul would never say that because I've never been married before him. He was my first and only husband.

October 1992

He leapt up and started dancing around the room, naked.

'What's that?' I said. 'A jig?'

'Something like one,' he said.

He twirled swiftly on sure feet. I leant on one elbow and watched. He had hairy legs and a lovely grin.

'You're all jiggling about,' I said.

He grabbed a towel and wrapped it round his waist. He continued to waltz. I got up.

'Would you like a cuppa?' I asked.

He nodded and swung out of the lounge. The flat was a studio, with a sofa bed in the large lounge. The walls were painted a soft lemon so the flat always seemed sunny and warm, even on dark days. The kitchen and bathroom were separate rooms. Even though the flat was a small space by conventional standards, it had a light, spacious feel about it. It had large windows at the front looking out over Roehampton and, to the right, in the distance, was Richmond Park. Behind us was Putney Heath with Barnes beyond. The flat also had a balcony – a summer place for sipping drinks and watching the city lights.

I went to the kitchen and put the kettle on. A new energy

surged through me. I hugged myself and slipped two teabags into two cups, poured water on them and added milk.

He came into the kitchen and kissed the back of my neck. He moved around me and looked out of the window.

'Oh what a lovely day,' he said.

I joined him. The rain was smashing against the window and London was a grey gloom. I heard one of the plant pots on the balcony rocking in its saucer. I looked at him. He had a broad grin. He picked up his cup of tea and took a sip.

'Yugh.' He put it down. 'I can't drink this,' he said.

'Why not?' I said.

'It tastes like drain water. Don't you know how to make a cup of tea?'

'I thought I did,' I said.

He tipped his cup of tea and my cup of tea down the sink. I felt the hair on my neck rising. I bit my lip.

'Start again,' he said.

I watched as he put the kettle on, took out two new cups, put a tea bag in each of them and poured boiling water on them. He got a spoon and gently squished each bag against the side of each cup. The tea merged with the hot water, dark, rich brown. He waited.

'Brew,' he said in his light Scottish accent.

'Ooch,' I said, 'a wee brew. Is it ready now?'

He nodded. I took my cup and sipped: it tasted good. He sipped his and we looked at each other.

'There, that's how I like my tea.'

'You're bossy,' I said.

He picked up his cup and sprang out of the kitchen. The wind rattled the building. He looked at the telephone on a small table.

'Can I call my family?' he asked.

'Yes, of course.'

I sat next to him on the sofa. He felt so familiar, as if I had known him a long time. He dialled a number; someone answered.

'Mam,' he exclaimed, 'I'm with Jill.'

I listened as he chatted excitedly to his mother, recounting the events of his week. He did not say much about me so I suspected he had already told his family.

'Would you like to talk to her?' he asked me.

Startled at his request, I nodded and took the receiver. A kind, gentle voice greeted me.

'Hello, Jill, lovely to talk to you.'

'Yes.'

'Where are you from?'

'Yorkshire.'

'Well, you know what they say about Yorkshire people.'

'No.'

'You can never take the Yorkshire out of a Yorkshire person. I had a lovely neighbour once, she was from Barnsley. She made me beautiful Yorkshire puddings. What are yours like?'

'I get them from the supermarket, I'm ashamed to admit.'

'You young people are all so busy.'

'It's all convenience now.'

'I'm really looking forward to meeting you.'

I looked over at him: he was pretending not to listen.

'Me too.' I handed the receiver back to Paul and he continued his conversation, now with his father. Laughter filled the room.

Tape 6: 25 January 2004: 13.27–14.10 continued

DC Bosomworth I just want to cover any cards that Paul's mother, Isla, may have sent or other keepsakes before her death in 1999.

JA   Yes.

DC Bosomworth   I'll ask that question again: do you possess or have you retained?

JA   I think I've kept two or three very special letters that are personal to me. I can certainly provide you with the originals or copies, more than happy to.

DC Bosomworth   Do you possess them at this time?

JA   Yes.

DC Bosomworth   I'll ask that question again: do you possess or have you retained?

JA   Yes.

DC Bosomworth   Right, OK, and they are letters regarding what?

JA   All the beautiful things she used to say to us. Just what's going on in their lives and about the family and, just lovely things.

DC Bosomworth   In any of those letters or correspondence to yourself and Paul, did she ever refer to Paul's illness?

JA   I don't recall but she gave us a lot of support.

DC Bosomworth   Right.

JA   A lot of support. She was constantly suggesting things and she asked about his symptoms. At this point in time we hadn't really got a diagnosis. We'd just got post-viral disability. She was trying to understand and help us.

DC Bosomworth   Right.

JA   She also said to us that she understood why we hadn't been to visit them in Scotland and she was just wonderful. She said all the right things. All you would expect from your family in this situation we found ourselves in. It was real and true love.

November 1998

The shop in Northallerton was like stepping back in time to the 1930s. The hardware it sold was designed to survive and be functional through an entire lifecycle, from marriage to death, and then passed on to the next generation. At the entrance, displayed on the pavement, were a smorgasbord of wicker baskets, stiff, hard brooms and plants. The shop itself was long and narrow, with short flights of steps linking several different levels. At the front was a gardener's paradise, with all manner of twine, trowels, buckets, forks, spades, hosepipes and paraphernalia. We would spend what seemed like hours picking the packets of seeds up from their racks, our mouths watering as we read about each vegetable variety and the scents of the sweetpeas. Beyond the gardening section were all the DIY materials, with nails and screws neatly labelled in cardboard boxes on shelves that reached to the ceiling.

We were standing at the far end of the shop. It had taken us some time to work our way to the back. There were shining copper kettles ready to nestle in the stonework of a Yorkshire fireplace. There were bone china dinner services, steamers, every utensil possible or imaginable, trays moulded for buns and tubes of paper to pour the mixture into the paper cases. We made our selection, a glazed beige mixing bowl with a pie-crust border. Amid much laughter, the owner, an elderly man with pince-nez balanced on his nose, took our money and rang up the transaction on an old-fashioned till. His wife, a blancmange of curves, put the bowl into a brown paper bag for us.

Night was falling as we left the shop. It was a chill Saturday in November, and we turned up the collars of our jackets and wrapped our scarves more tightly. The odd few leaves left over from their autumn fall skittered down the street around our feet as we made for the car. People were darting in huddled clusters, rushing to get home. We were homeward bound, too.

Later he made some lemon cakes. Delicious.

What actually caused Paul Anderson's death was morphine poisoning, so in one view, he caused his death by his own act and it was the morphine that led to his death. An overdose of morphine can be treated quite simply, so the failure to summon medical assistance was very, very serious in this case, because of the risk of death. It is inconceivable that she did not realize that Paul Anderson had taken a serious overdose.

It was obvious that the failure to carry out that simple act carried with it a serious risk of death, and that failure – the simple failure – to perform a simple act that would have saved a life was, in those circumstances that I have described, grossly negligent.

From the Prosecution's closing speech

Tape 6: 25 January 2004: 13.27–14.10 continued

DC Bosomworth	Other than Isla's letters or correspondence with yourself, Paul and his sister's letters as well, did any of Paul's family ever correspond with you during his illness?
JA	No. I don't recall that.
DC Bosomworth	I know that you obviously spoke on the telephone.

JA   Yes and then we got Christmas presents and
                      cards and things initially. Isla and I had a
                      writing relationship. I wrote letters to her.
                      We have got some copies of those on the
                      Apple Mac on a hard drive. Letters that I
                      sent.

DC Bosomworth What about Paul's birthdays and Christmas?
                      You mentioned cards, were they regularly
                      sent from his family or were there people
                      who deliberately did not send cards or pres-
                      ents?

JA   He got cards regularly until the rift and then
                      they all stopped.

DC Bosomworth They stopped? Every one?

JA   Yes, I think so. I mean some people would
                      forget now and again. It doesn't matter, does
                      it?

DC Bosomworth Other than his eldest sister, was there any
                      other member of Paul's family that
                      attempted to build bridges via letters or tele-
                      phone?

JA   His younger sister called us in the summer of
                      2001 and it just ended up in another argument
                      and we didn't want to argue with them.

DC Bosomworth Was this over the telephone?

JA   Yes.

DC Bosomworth Right, anything through written word or
                      anything like that?

JA   No.

DC Bosomworth Was Paul aware of these contacts?

JA   Oh yes.

DC Bosomworth To your knowledge then, who was the last

person that Paul spoke to regarding his family.

JA   Probably his brother.

DC Bosomworth   Did you ever stop his father bringing down a Christmas present for you and Paul?

JA   He wanted to come down and visit us just before Christmas. Paul had Irritable Bowel Syndrome.

DC Bosomworth   No, that's all right, you've clarified that, that's OK. I'm going to move on slightly and I'm going to move to the day you viewed Paul's body, which was the 21st of July.

JA   Yes.

DC Bosomworth   2003, I think. Did you go with your mum?

JA   Yes, I did.

DC Bosomworth   I have a statement from an Anatomical Pathology Technician who was present when you attended with your mother and she told us that you said words to the effect of, 'He's been in terrible pain for years, we've tried everything for it but this time it's been sorted out.' Do you recollect saying that?

JA   No, I never said that. I will have said he's been in terrible pain for years, but I would not have made the last statement, no.

DC Bosomworth   Well, I wasn't there and it isn't something I've made up. It's information that's come to me.

JA   I would not say that.

DC Bosomworth   So you didn't say?

JA   Do you want to repeat that sentence again?

DC Bosomworth   I'll do it all for you. 'He's been in terrible

	pain for years, we've tried everything for it but this time it's been sorted out.'
JA	No, I wouldn't say, 'this time it's been sorted out', no. The first two sentences, yes, definitely, but not, 'this time it's been sorted out'.
DC Bosomworth	Have you said anything that could have been misconstrued?
JA	I think we all do, absolutely. I mean, we try our best to communicate.
DC Bosomworth	Because, to be fair, it's a peculiar thing for somebody to say, or a peculiar thing for somebody to allege to say, 'this time it's been sorted out'.
JA	I would never say it.
DC Bosomworth	On the 29th July you enquired with Police Constable Day regarding the release of the body for the funeral.
JA	Was he based at the coroner's office?
DC Bosomworth	No, he wasn't. He was based at Ripon, actually.
Solicitor	So, would this be a telephone call, then?
DC Bosomworth	Yes, right. And what he told me is that you asked him if he would look at everything in his system. Have you asked that of the police officer?
JA	I might have done.
DC Bosomworth	Well, would you have a reason to ask that?
JA	I wanted to know how he died.
DC Bosomworth	Right. What did you expect them to find in his system?
JA	All the pills he had taken.
DC Bosomworth	And what pills did he have?

JA	He had a whole combination but there was morphine and Zopiclone and a whole drawer full of medication that had gathered over the years. Normally he would try medication for three weeks and then discontinue it, which exactly matches clinical trials.
DC Bosomworth	Other than prescribed medicines from his doctor, what over-the-counter remedies did he use?
JA	All kinds. He just told me what he'd like to try and I went and got it for him.
DC Bosomworth	Right, so what medication? Would he have, for example, over-the-counter pills for rheumatoid arthritis?
JA	I think there's something called sepia, herbal remedies. He tried Qualms [sic], the herbal sleeping remedy. He tried devil's claw.
DC Bosomworth	What's devil's claw?
JA	It's a sleeping remedy for rheumatoid arthritis, pain relief. It's in Boots. We went through the whole selection of medications over the counter because he was desperate to relieve the pain that he was experiencing physically.
DC Bosomworth	According to PC Day, you also asked him if they would look into his financial situation. Why have you asked that question?
JA	I've no idea. I can't imagine why on earth I would say that.
DC Bosomworth	Do you remember asking that?
JA	No.
DC Bosomworth	Do you deny asking that?
JA	I've no idea whether I asked it or not.

August 1993

A large spider walked into the room at Lime Court. It moved closer to us as we sat on the sofa among books and magazines.

'Do something,' I said.

'What, it's just a spider.'

'They bite. What if it comes into the bed at night?'

'You're bigger than it.'

'It has to go,' I said.

'You'd probably roll over and squash it,' he replied.

'I won't be able to sleep.'

The spider was coming closer to us, negotiating the eastern boundary of the flat, hugging the wall, moving in quick starts and then stopping. Paul put down the magazine he was reading.

'Where's the dustpan?' he said.

'Under the sink.'

Paul went into the kitchen and started rummaging in the cupboard. The spider changed direction and started walking diagonally across the room.

'Hurry, it's crossing the border.' Our flat was on the border of Putney and Barnes, so I liked to think the dividing line ran through our living room. 'It's moved over into Barnes.'

'Maybe it will be happy in Barnes,' Paul said, returning from the kitchen with the dustpan and brush. The spider moved rapidly across the room and disappeared under one of the tables. Paul went over to where it had last been sighted and moved the table to one side. He bent over and scooped.

'Open the balcony door,' he said.

I went ahead of him and swung the door open. Paul tipped the dustpan gently so the spider slid smoothly onto the patio. We watched as it shuffled to the edge of the balcony and disappeared from view. I turned to him.

'I don't like spiders.'

'Arachnids,' he replied.

'Spiders.'

'Let's go to the video shop and get a creepy-crawly movie out tonight.' He grinned. His eyes were bright and sparkling.

'Whatever,' I replied.

We returned to the sofa and sat together, reading. I felt something on my neck, fingers going up and down.

'You.' I smacked his hand.

'Spider,' he said.

'Don't ever leave me.'

Tape 6: 25 January 2004: 13.27–14.10 continued

DC Bosomworth	And you actually said to PC Boulton, you returned at 1800 hours. Again, I'm not too bothered about whether it was 6 or half past.
JA	I don't know.
DC Bosomworth	But you told her, 'I thought he'd taken enough this time.' What did you mean by that?
JA	No, just a moment, can I just stop the interview and ask my solicitor a question?
DC Bosomworth	We'll have to close the interview if you want to.
Solicitor	If you're happy to come back to that, I . . .
DC Bosomworth	I'll come back.
JA	I have the exact words, but I need to check them with my solicitor first.
Solicitor	Right, that's fine.
DC Bosomworth	I'll come back to that then.
Solicitor	Thank you.
DC Bosomworth	You told PC Boulton, when she asked,

'When did you know he had passed away?'
You replied, 'Five o'clock in the morning' or
'Five o'clock this morning.'

JA   No, he died at 9.30.

DC Bosomworth   So, why did you say 5 o'clock?

JA   She must have misheard me. He went blue
about 5 or 6 a.m.

DC Bosomworth   So how did you know when he'd died?

JA   I heard his last breath.

DC Bosomworth   And originally, when PC Boulton was com-
pleting the sudden death report, which we
have, you stated you discovered your husband
dead at 10 a.m. What were the circumstances
in discovering your husband dead?

JA   No. I discovered him at 9.30. I went up to see
him.

DC Bosomworth   So if you went up to see him at 9.30, when
was the last time you saw him prior to that?

JA   I was with him all night, backwards and forwards.

DC Bosomworth   Sorry.

JA   I can't give you an answer on that. Can we
come back to that?

DC Bosomworth   Is that because you want to discuss it with
your solicitor?

JA   Yes, it is.

DC Bosomworth   Or, you can't remember?

JA   I was in the house with him. He was in crip-
pling pain. I'd started sleeping downstairs
because I couldn't even hug him anymore.

DC Bosomworth   Shall we let you have your talk with your
solicitor on that one?

JA	Yes.
DC Bosomworth	OK. Did you make any phone calls from the house on the 18th, or the morning of the 18th?
JA	Yes, I did. I called his GP.
DC Bosomworth	Anybody else?
JA	I don't remember.
DC Bosomworth	Did anybody else make phone calls from your house that morning?
JA	Well, it'd just be me.
DC Bosomworth	Some of the stuff we've covered before, but I'd like to get one or two things clear into my head. How did you actually see your role as Paul Anderson's carer?
JA	I was devoted to him. I loved every single hair of him, every single molecule and every single cell in his body. I was completely devoted to him.
DC Bosomworth	And what did you see your responsibilities as, then?
JA	Taking care of him, ensuring that he could stay alive, making everything possible for him to get well. It's the only reason we moved to the cottage, to give him a healthy environment. I did everything.

Each of us has various rights. The right to a family life; the right to freedom of expression; the right to go out to work; the right to do all sorts of things; and one of the rights that each of us has is the right to determine his – or her – own life, and that includes the right to choose to die.

From the Defence's closing speech

Tape 6: 25 January 2004: 13.27–14.10 continued

DC Bosomworth Did you have to, for example, bath him?

JA Towards the end, his bath time was the most personal, private time of his day. It's the only time he never wanted to be disturbed and I respected that. Now I don't understand, and this is a question I ask myself, because I know his arms were getting weaker, why he didn't ask me to help him, but he didn't.

DC Bosomworth Right.

JA Because he was a man and he was concerned about me. He loved me and he was trying to cope with this terrible illness and make it as easy as possible for me as his carer.

DC Bosomworth So regarding dressing himself, could he dress himself?

JA He could, just about.

DC Bosomworth Combing of the hair.

JA He hated that, but I'd do anything for him, anything he asked.

DC Bosomworth But could he do these things for himself, Jill, is what I'm asking you?

JA Towards the end he couldn't lift his arms at the back like this.

DC Bosomworth You've indicated like a brushing motion towards the back of the head.

JA That's right.

DC Bosomworth With your right arm, yeah.

JA Yes.

DC Bosomworth So he couldn't do that?

JA   He could only do this.

DC Bosomworth So you're saying, it's like eating with a knife and fork, if you like.

JA   Yes, or writing or holding something.

DC Bosomworth Right.

JA   Because I would comb his hair for him.

DC Bosomworth Could he take the top off of his medication, for example?

JA   Yes, he'd be able to do that.

DC Bosomworth Could he open the packaging?

JA   Yes.

DC Bosomworth I have seen the authority and you have actually said that you discussed his illness with his GP.

JA   I'd tell them what he had asked for. He was asking, not me. He had suggested the medication and then I'd go and collect it for him.

DC Bosomworth But you arranged that with the doctor yourself?

JA   Yes, because Paul was too ill to get on the phone and do that for himself, so he told me and I relayed his messages.

DC Bosomworth Did you actually suggest to the doctor any medication that Paul should be taking?

JA   Yes, I found some information on the Internet about these painkillers that were helping people with Chronic Fatigue Syndrome, because I discussed it with Paul and Paul wanted to try it. It was Paul's decision.

DC Bosomworth Which was?

JA   The opiates.

DC Bosomworth What, the morphine?

JA Yes, there are four different types and there was an article on the Internet from a Chronic Fatigue doctor in America who'd had some success with reducing the pain, then people could come back up again. They made some kind of recovery. Every day I told him he would get better. Every day we told each other we loved each other about seventeen times a day, that's the relationship we had.

February 1993

I ran down Roehampton Lane in what seemed like a force 10 gale. My umbrella blew inside out. I had to get home to him. I wondered if he had arrived back from his shift. I looked up through layers of rain at our flat in Lime Court to see if the light was on. I reached our front door, opened it and shoved the umbrella into a pot that held my jade plant, an old curled friend, and went into the lounge. He was there, on the sofa, his work clothes in a heap on the floor. I pulled off my mac, adding it to the heap, and joined him.

'Nice day?' he said.

'No, horrible,' I replied.

We munched on some crisps. He was watching the evening news on television.

'Anyone dead?' I said.

'President of an African country, coup d'état. Do you have to crunch so loudly?'

'Any floods, tornadoes?'

'Nah.'

'Shark attacks?'

'No.'

'How was your day?'

'Horrible,' he said. 'Are you going to put your mac away?'

'Are you going to clear up your heap?' I replied.

'Don't you think you should put your mac away? I don't want to break my neck.'

I looked at him: he had a sparkle in his eye. I picked up the mac, opened the door to my closet and stood back. There was a large bouquet of bright, bright red roses and a card. I grabbed them. Smelt them.

'Happy Valentine's Day, darling bear,' he said.

'Your turn,' I said.

He went to his closet and found my gift. He ripped it open: I had given him a book voucher.

'You had me on edge all day. I thought you'd forgotten,' I said.

Tape 6: 25 January 2004: 13.27–14.10 continued

DC Bosomworth	So you asked the doctor for this, on Paul's behalf?
JA	Yes, but Paul asked me.
DC Bosomworth	Yeah, I appreciate that, Jill, but you asked the doctor for it on Paul's behalf?
JA	Yes. And we issued a letter signed jointly by us saying that Paul was giving me permission to speak for him, as he was too ill to get to the telephone.
DC Bosomworth	Yes, we've seen the letter. We've seen it's jointly signed.
JA	Yes.

DC Bosomworth	And he gave you authority to discuss his illness?
JA	Yes.
DC Bosomworth	With his doctor?
JA	Yes, Paul was directing me. He was certainly ...
DC Bosomworth	Which I'm assuming.
JA	... involved in all the medication. He was making a lot of the suggestions. He was his own man.
DC Richardson	Did you ask for any government benefit for being his carer?
JA	I think I looked into it and we weren't entitled. I can't remember all the logistics.
Solicitor	It's a carer's allowance, isn't it?
JA	Yes.
Solicitor	Right.
JA	So, we looked into it. If you earn so much money then they won't give it to you. I think because I was working then you can't receive carer's allowance, something like that.
DC Richardson	Well, you can't have both really.
JA	That's right. I don't recall, but we did look into it, obviously ...
DC Richardson	Did you actually apply for it then, Jill, or not?
JA	No, but obviously we probably discussed it with the ME Association because they're set up to try and give people advice.
DC Richardson	Right, are you a member of the ME Association?
JA	I'm not. I didn't join, but it has always been my intention to join.

DC Richardson	Did you get any other assistance from the local authority?
JA	Yes, we got our council tax paid for a short period of time.
DC Richardson	Is that because of Paul's illness?
JA	Yes.
DC Richardson	And not necessarily anything to do with you being his carer?
JA	No, it was Paul's illness.
DC Richardson	Any disability benefit?
JA	On the day he died, he took his own life, we'd started filling out a disability form.
DC Richardson	That was the claim you were going to actually make then, wasn't it?
JA	Yes.
DC Richardson	And what would the claim have entailed then? I mean, I've never claimed, I wouldn't know because I'm obviously not disabled.
JA	Yes.
DC Richardson	And I don't have any relatives who are disabled.
JA	Yes.
DC Richardson	So I've had no reason to make a claim, if you like, so I don't know what the form consists of. I don't know the procedure.
JA	Well, you just ...
DC Richardson	Claim.
JA	Fill out a big form and then send it off to ... I can't remember, I don't know who you send it off to but ...
DC Richardson	Right.

JA	The address is on the form and we'd then . . .
DC Richardson	And did you have that form then, Jill?
JA	Yes, we were filling it out on the day he took his own life.
DC Richardson	And did you put yourself down as his carer on that form?
JA	I don't know whether that is a section on the form.
DC Richardson	I don't know the form.
JA	No, I don't know whether they have a section for the carer.
DC Richardson	But . . .
JA	But, I was his carer.
DC Richardson	You would think if somebody was applying for disabled benefit there would be a section there to say who was looking after them though, wouldn't you?
JA	Probably, yes there must be. I would think but I . . .
DC Richardson	Were you just thinking logically?
JA	Yes, I was. By that time I was self-employed and not entitled to a single bean for being his carer. You can look into it, if you're self-employed, which is fair enough. I agree with that.
DC Richardson	OK.
JA	I'd rather, you know, we wanted to be, obviously, independent of the state.
DC Richardson	My colleague mentioned that in 1995, no '98, I think you tried claiming in '95. Was there something from the Citizen's Advice Bureau? Did you go to them at all?

JA	No idea, I can't remember because we were working in 1995.
DC Richardson	Were you?
JA	We worked on our business from '94 to '98 and then we went bankrupt.
DC Richardson	Right.
JA	And we were tax payers, so I can't understand why we would look into it then, plus he wasn't so ill then.
DC Richardson	Right.
JA	So there wouldn't be any reason to do that?
DC Richardson	Did you go to the Citizen's Advice Bureau?
JA	I went twice, in Ripon, in 2003, to talk about disability.
DC Richardson	I assume about Paul's disability?
JA	Yes.
DC Richardson	And that you had to care for him?
JA	I was obviously his carer, otherwise I wouldn't be there. I was taking care of him. He needed the form and I'd heard from the ME Association. They said, if you're filling out a form for disability go to your local Citizen's Advice Bureau because they know how to fill out these forms correctly, that's why we went.
DC Richardson	I'm assuming you needed some form of help, whether it be financial?
JA	Of course. He couldn't support me as a husband and a fully-able man.
DC Richardson	How do you feel about that?
JA	It was a privilege and an honour to take care of him. I have never seen someone suffer so

	quietly and so patiently with such a dreadful illness. He made me laugh every day of his life.
DC Richardson	So, other than that, Jill, there was no financial gain in being his carer then?
JA	No.
DC Richardson	To you, I mean?
JA	No.
DC Richardson	No.
JA	There's no financial gain to being a carer, very little reward.
DC Richardson	We've mentioned briefly to your solicitor, and indeed he has intimated, that you'd have no objections to us examining your medical records and your bank details. Does that still stand?
JA	Yes.
DC Richardson	OK. John, over to you.
DC Bosomworth	Just going into that subject, Jill, of bank details. Obviously you ran a business. You had a business account.
JA	Yes.
DC Bosomworth	Is that fair to say? Did you have personal accounts?
JA	Yes, I've got a personal account.
DC Bosomworth	Not necessarily now, but whilst you were with Paul, did you have a personal account away from Paul, i.e. not a joint account?
JA	That's right.
DC Bosomworth	Did you have a joint account?
JA	No.
DC Bosomworth	Did Paul have his own account?

JA	Yes.
DC Bosomworth	So there's a business account and two other accounts: one for you and one for Paul?
JA	Yes.
DC Bosomworth	Were they deposit accounts, your personal ones, or current?
JA	Current.
DC Bosomworth	Both current.
JA	Yes. There is no money so you're very welcome to look.
DC Bosomworth	Right. So there's no money in either account, Paul's or yourself?
JA	No.
DC Bosomworth	Possessions of Paul, were there many?
JA	No, everything we owned was joint, everything. I've just got his personal possessions with me.
DC Bosomworth	His personal effects?
JA	Yes, his binoculars, his guitar.
DC Bosomworth	Right.
JA	His walking boots, his books, his dictionaries.

November 1995

We arrived at the car park for Gouthwaite Reservoir just to the north of Pateley Bridge. In the years to come, we would visit this place many times, birdwatching and spending time together. We would eventually own 'his and hers' binoculars, but today we shared Paul's pair. The car park had a picnic area where we ate our crisps and sandwiches in silence, then we crossed the road to the hide. It was surrounded by a high hedge, secluding it from the road like a small square of maze. We stepped through the doorway in the hedge and onto wooden decking that stretched out over the water.

The wide mirror of the lake stretched in front of us, with woods and hills rolling to the horizon beyond. The sun shone: Paul directed the binoculars away from its glare and did a sweep of the water. He gave me a list of the birds he could see: Canada geese, goosanders, mallards, tufted ducks and whooper swans were on the water. Then he added, 'I can see grey herons.'

'Where?' I said.

'To the left.'

I squinted. 'Can I have the binoculars?' I asked.

Paul handed them over to me. Sure enough, there in the reeds on the far shore I could make out six or seven herons, spaced apart, in their own sections of reeds. They either had their long necks stretched out and were motionless, waiting patiently for their prey, fish or an eel, or were resting with their necks bent down over their chests.

We decided to go over to the other side of the reservoir to see if we could get closer to the herons. It was a drive and a walk to where a public footpath ran along the side. About an hour and a half later, we had reached the place we had intended, but there was a fence that prevented walkers going down to the shore with a sign stating 'NO TRESPASSERS'. We looked at each other.

'There's no one around,' I said.

'We shouldn't,' he said.

'I know.'

We stood undecided. The herons and their proximity to us were on our minds. We surveyed the vicinity again: mid-afternoon and silence. We clambered over the fence quickly, and furtively ran down to the shore and a screen of trees. We thudded ourselves down on the bank then shuffled down the shale on the shoreline so no one could see us from the path. Paul directed the binoculars to where we knew the herons were. A few minutes later he handed them to me.

'If . . .' he said.

'Yes.'

'If a park ranger approaches us we'll pretend to be from another country. I'll speak to him in Russian.'

'Good idea,' I said. 'It could be a she.'

Paul arched an eyebrow. 'You say nothing,' he said.

'All right, comrade,' I replied.

We settled down and continued sharing the binoculars. Twenty minutes later we clambered back over the fence, looking around to see if anyone had seen us, but the path remained free of visitors. We hugged and casually strolled away from the scene of our crime, whistling.

Towards the end, I would walk at Gouthwaite alone and return to the cottage to tell him the herons were still wading. I would take his binoculars, more powerful than mine. He would smile, reaching out his hand to me. I would take it and run my fingers over his. He would look in his bedside cabinet, where he kept his bird books in the top drawer, with all his medication, and place them on the bed before us. We would find the section on herons and reread it together.

Tape 6: 25 January 2004: 13.27–14.10 continued

DC Bosomworth	Were there any serious assets like shares or . . . ?
JA	No.
DC Bosomworth	Large properties or anything else like that?
JA	No, none.
DC Bosomworth	Nothing.

JA	None whatsoever. We fell off the ladder. We couldn't get a mortgage.
DC Bosomworth	And that was down to Paul's illness?
JA	Yes.
DC Bosomworth	And not being able to earn money. Is that correct?
JA	That's right.
DC Bosomworth	OK.
JA	We went bankrupt and lost our credit rating.
DC Bosomworth	We've been talking to you about your role as a carer.
JA	Yes.
DC Bosomworth	And going through it in detail. You were telling him about it and at one point you got very angry.
JA	Yes.
DC Bosomworth	And you said the words that you stood up to anyone who said it wasn't a virus.
JA	Stand up. I tried to do it very gently and politely and professionally with everyone who I encountered, including his own family, that he had a virus, he wasn't mentally ill.
DC Bosomworth	I appreciate that. Were you, how can I put it, abusive to his family?
JA	I don't believe in abusing people. I try to do things professionally. Now, I might lose my temper and be snippy. I don't say nasty things to people. I don't see the point. I don't see what it achieves. I don't understand character assassination or pulling people to shreds. I try to give facts and then leave people to

assess those facts, but I'm renowned as an incredibly kind, gentle person.

DC Bosomworth Did you see yourself in, sort of, a siege mentality with Paul and other people's opinions of his disease?

JA To an extent, but I couldn't be responsible for their opinions. I could only give the facts and the truth. We had a wonderful marriage. It wasn't how we wanted. The cottage was purely for peace and quiet. It was a wonderful healthy environment which we both enjoyed. The families could be difficult. I tried to give them facts. You've heard about Paul's family. Other than that we had just amazing friendships and emails.

DC Bosomworth You did have friendships in other countries, didn't you? I've noticed that from the computer.

JA Yes, gifts came from friends every week. Our lives were filled with people.

DC Bosomworth You did have people who were sympathetic to you.

JA Oh, yes.

DC Bosomworth And what was going on?

JA Who believed us.

DC Bosomworth But then again you also had people who were close family who didn't.

JA Yes.

DC Bosomworth You also had a good relationship with Paul.

JA Yes.

DC Bosomworth Why did you care about what the family felt?

JA	Because we moved to Yorkshire to be close to the family.
DC Bosomworth	And obviously that didn't work out?
JA	It destroyed us. It was heartbreaking what they said to us.
DC Bosomworth	How did you deal with this then, personally, how did you deal with it?
JA	I got constant support from the ME Association and the Carer's Resource and friends, that's how I dealt with it.
DC Bosomworth	Because we spoke about medical records, were you seeing a doctor to assist you through these times?
JA	I went and got counselling at the GP surgery. In fact, let's start earlier than that. I saw a doctor at Pateley Bridge. She's a psychiatrist. I talked to her about our situation and these are the words she gave me. 'Paul comes first, do your best, ignore them.' I also had counselling at the GP surgery in Ripon. I went for one and a half sessions. Halfway through the second session she said, Jill, you and Paul are doing absolutely fantastic, you don't need to see me anymore, because normally you would go for six sessions. She said, you're coping really well.
DC Bosomworth	And did you agree with that?
JA	Yes, I did.
DC Bosomworth	So you were happy with the way you were dealing with things. I know you were obviously dealing with your husband's illness, but I'm talking about things within and without, regarding family.

JA	I tried to do my best.
DC Bosomworth	Right.
JA	I felt that I was doing that and other people said that I was just trying to do my best.
DC Bosomworth	Because it seems, aside from the internet, your business and the like, that you were entrenched. There were outside forces, but most, or the closest people, which could be, you know, your family, your immediate family and Paul's immediate family, didn't believe you. You said you stood up to anybody who said it wasn't a virus. Did you take this as a crusade?
JA	No, I think that's the wrong word. Stood up, presented facts, crusade to an extent, yes, to get the information across to people to make it better for other people.
DC Bosomworth	I appreciate you know that, when people approach you and say, 'I don't believe it,' then you're going to stand up for Paul. But were you actually taking those facts to people and saying, look, I know you haven't said anything for the last X amount of months, but this is what happened? This is what this disease is about. That's what I mean by presenting a crusade. Were you confronting people, unsolicited, with the information?
JA	Unsolicited. I'd make an appointment to see a GP, that's not unsolicited.
DC Bosomworth	Sorry, I'm talking about family now or people who didn't believe you.
JA	No, in actual fact, the ME Association said

	why don't you send them some literature. I didn't, because I felt it was their responsibility to ask for the literature. It wasn't my responsibility. I'd asked them to consider Chronic Fatigue Syndrome and they didn't.
DC Bosomworth	Right.
JA	I can only do so much for people.
DC Bosomworth	You didn't approach any members of the family without them asking for . . . ?
JA	No.
DC Bosomworth	Information, with information.
JA	No.
DC Bosomworth	Right.
JA	I don't believe that that's up to me. That's propaganda and dictatorship and I don't do that.
DC Bosomworth	Some people don't and I don't know yet, so . . .
JA	Yes.
DC Bosomworth	That's why I'm asking.
JA	No, I try to be lenient with people and tolerant and give them their right to their own point of view. Me and Paul, you say it was a siege mentality. It wasn't. We were just in the cottage dealing with a very serious illness having a very nice time because we loved each other and our days were spent in laughter. We were forced to adopt a lifestyle that we didn't want. We did not ask for this terrible virus, biological warfare, we had to develop our own life. I know that outsiders might see it differently, but it's how we dealt

with the fact that my husband did not have a
body. He did not have a body that worked
anymore. So, how do you have a social life?
All he wanted to do was take me to the
cinema, go to the theatre, all the things we
did in London, such as parties, and visiting
friends. We couldn't do it. So he did wood-
work when he could because it doesn't hurt
anyone. I did gardening because gardening
doesn't hurt anyone. Our lives were not
about hurting people.

DC Bosomworth Who would you tell then, other than family
and doctors et cetera, that Paul was ill?

JA   All our friends and we have close friends in
England as well.

DC Bosomworth Right.

JA   Very close.

DC Bosomworth I'm not disputing that ...

JA   No.

DC Bosomworth It's just that I've noticed this on the ...

JA   Oh yeah.

DC Bosomworth ... on the emails.

JA   I can tell you about the visitors we had to the
cottage in the period of time we were there.
We had two friends from the States. Alex
Rainer and her husband, Roland. They came
to visit the cottage and we had a wonderful
time with them. Paul was well enough to
spend a bit of time with them. They came
twice.

DC Bosomworth When was that, then?

JA   This was, I don't know, in 2000 or 2001, then we had some more friends that came to visit. Lorraine, Al and her family.

DC Bosomworth Didn't you consider then, obviously, Paul's family, who loved Paul?

JA They said they loved him but I don't think it's love because . . .

DC Bosomworth But is that for you to decide? Is that your place to decide that they . . . ?

JA I didn't decide that. He did.

DC Bosomworth OK.

JA I said to his father, we need you. I begged him.

DC Bosomworth So this would have been happening in 2000, around the time your American friends came across?

JA Yes, I mean, people came to the cottage, you know, friends came to the cottage. It was Paul's decision, because we could not argue with them anymore.

DC Bosomworth That's . . .

JA So, are you suggesting then? I'm just saying that the relationship between his father and his brother was so antagonistic that we had to walk away from them.

DC Bosomworth Did his eldest sister ever speak to you, for instance? I'm just picking a name.

JA Oh well, it's a long time, you know.

DC Bosomworth Did she ever express a wish to visit Paul?

JA I, you know . . .

Solicitor Well, we've dealt with this in the . . .

JA Yes, we've dealt with this.

Solicitor In the other interview. I don't want to be here all day . . .

JA	And this is a fact.
Solicitor	. . . covering the same ground.
DC Bosomworth	I think I'll ask the question.
JA	This is very difficult because all Paul and I wanted was for them to come and see him, to have a nice family relationship.
DC Bosomworth	Why I asked this . . .
JA	And it didn't happen because they didn't believe him.
DC Bosomworth	It is because you mentioned that your American friends were able to visit Paul. That Paul was going through a good period in his illness, if you like?
JA	Yes.
DC Bosomworth	He was able to see them?
JA	Yes.
DC Bosomworth	Didn't it occur to you or Paul to contact his family whilst he was going through a similar period?
JA	No, because they argued with us. I was frightened of his brother.
DC Bosomworth	What about his elder sister, for instance?
JA	Well, it was four against one and we've discussed this. It was four against one. This was Paul's decision. I can't go back over this with you. These are people that did not believe in Chronic Fatigue Syndrome. They thought he was mentally ill. I just found, in terms of what I was doing and achieving, I found their relationships impossible to deal with and so did he, but it was him and his decision.
DC Bosomworth	His decision.

JA   I backed him up as his wife.

DC Bosomworth   Did you, at any time, make decisions regard-
                      ing say phoning up family to visit him when
                      he was going through a good period, or was
                      it Paul's decision?

JA   It was Paul's decision and I talked to his
                      father for a year at the cottage. Paul was too
                      ill to see him and Chronic Fatigue Syndrome
                      goes up and down. When our American
                      friends came he was able to get up and see
                      them for a few hours. Then, he went back to
                      bed and I took them out to a restaurant. He
                      couldn't come to the restaurant with us for
                      the meal.

DC Bosomworth   OK.

JA   They were fantastic and they gave him the
                      support that he needed and all they said to
                      him was, 'Our hearts go out to you.' That
                      was all he needed, but we weren't getting that
                      from his own family. You have talked to them
                      and it's vitriol and it's not fair. This is four
                      against one. I'm the only one left now of the
                      couple. Paul's not here to defend himself.

DC Bosomworth   Just, very briefly, there's about four minutes
                      left on the tape. In the very first interview we
                      had with you, you mentioned that Paul was
                      having cognitive behavioural therapy at
                      home?

JA   He did his own cognitive behaviour therapy.

DC Bosomworth   Right, did you assist with that?

JA   No.

DC Bosomworth   Was this agreed with the GP?

JA   No.

DC Bosomworth   So it was something he decided himself, was it?

JA   Yes.

DC Bosomworth   OK. You also stated.

JA   I'm sorry, that is, you do realize that's a mis-interpretation?

DC Bosomworth   Well, I think I've actually used your words, not mine.

JA   He made his . . .

DC Bosomworth   Because it's something I wouldn't know.

JA   He made his own flies for trout fishing.

DC Bosomworth   Yeah.

JA   Feathers and . . .

DC Bosomworth   Yeah, I know how to tie flies.

JA   That is cognitive behaviour therapy.

DC Bosomworth   Right.

October 2000

He watched me as I dressed. I was going to work in the office that we had made in the cottage on the lane with no name. The lane that reached all the way to the quiet limits of Pateley Moor and its wide spaces on the rooftop of the Pennines, that spine of hills that stretches up northern England. I turned to him.

'I need to lose weight.'

I imagined him thinking, I so need that problem. He never put on weight no matter what he ate: I was always envious.

He had his Italian dictionary on his knee, and had been running his finger down a list of words. I showed him my belly. His eyes glazed over. I cocked my head to one side waiting for a response.

'That's a nice kangaroo pouch, that is,' he said, returning to studying his dictionary. 'Can you get me the *Yeller*?'

I frowned. 'I'll try to remember.'

The *Yeller* was the free yellow newspaper of ads for anything anyone could possibly want. A few days later, I would finally remember to pick it up on one of my daily trips out. When I brought it to him, he started going through it until he found what he wanted. He circled three possibilities and asked me to make some phone calls. I relayed the conversations to him. The second call most closely fitted the requirements. I made the appointment and the next day he forced himself out. He dressed carefully and drove with me beside him. We found the address. It was a neat, tidy house on a busy street in downtown Leeds. A couple answered the door. They were in their early sixties.

'We're mostly retired,' the man of the house said.

He looked tired, his skin sallow and worn. The house was pristine and glamorous compared to the street outside. The walls all had beige, light brown or russet wallpaper or paint. Everything was coordinated.

'Our children have all gone,' his wife added. She had brightly dyed, red-brown hair.

'Yes, we want to get ready and get rid of stuff. We've got too much. It's time to clear out,' the man added convivially. 'Make the best of what's left.'

The man of the house showed it to Paul in the master bedroom, while I nattered with the wife in the kitchen. Paul snapped it up. It was a bargain – twenty-five quid. We drove home. He did not look at me as he drove. He knew I had my eyes shut. This was going to be another experience.

It took a few days, but then it was set up. The analogue satellite dish. He read more magazines and worked out the settings for the satellite in the sky. I held the stepladder so it did not rock.

'Can you put more weight on it?' he said.

I stamped my right foot down on the bottom rung and gripped the ladder more tightly. It was on the uneven surface of the yard, a mix of a botched concrete and gravel.

'Why are you taking so long?'

'I need to find the best point where it will get the strongest signal.'

I thought of all the other things I needed to do. He made criss-crosses in the place where he wanted to drill the holes and passed down the pencil and ruler. I passed up his drill. Shale fell on my head and shoulders like dandruff as he drilled the holes. I passed the brackets up to him and the ladder wobbled.

'Steady,' he shouted.

I passed the satellite dish up to him. He had drilled a hole in the window frame for the cables.

I heaved a sigh of relief as we went inside the cottage. My arms ached. He asked me to twist and turn the television in the bedroom as he stumbled back to the ladder and moved the dish slightly. I leaned out of the bedroom window to get his instructions, then I went back to the TV.

'Left a bit, no, no, right a bit, right a bit more, left again, just a smidge,' he barked.

He wanted to know when the picture was clear. We found it together, finally, after some time. Then he came inside and wrapped himself up with the manual. Later, he called me and showed me CNN, CBS, ABC and Turner Classic Movies. His face registered satisfaction.

The Al Gore versus George Bush election became a way to survive. A daily entertainment; a distraction to fill the void left by a real life with family and friends. The presenters on CNN became familiar to us. I would come in from the office and ask him, 'Is Wolf on?' We learnt all about chads: swinging chads, undecided chads, pregnant chads. Chads became our mantra and fixation. The map of the American states constantly alternated blue and red. Which state would go that way and would another state go another way? And when it all came down to the call in Florida we got excited. This was drama and connection. After it was all over and Bush had won, he turned to me and said, 'There'll be a lot of children in the States named Chad after this election.'

Two years later, I bought him a digital dish. Two lads from Sky came and set it up. He watched them as they fixed the second dish near to the first one. They chatted idly. One said his gig was to set up satellite dishes in the summer and go to Thailand in the winter with the earnings. Paul said that at some point we were going to move to the south of France, near the Pyrenees. It was one of our fantasies.

Cables ran all along the edge of the bedroom. I helped him hide them under the carpet like snakes in a nest. Then he would place a piece of paper on my pillow in the design of a cinema ticket, with the date and time of the movie he had found for us to watch in the evening. Often he would put on his favourite movie, *Die Hard*, and sing 'Let it snow, let it snow' to me as I flicked through a newspaper article or magazine. I got bored with *Die Hard* but it was his thing.

Tape 6: 25 January 2004: 13.27–14.10 continued

DC Bosomworth	OK. You stated that you begged the doctors for medication for him?
JA	Begged? I asked. I probably used the word begged too many times.
DC Bosomworth	Right.

JA	Again, this language, this English language that we use, can be twisted and turned. I'm trying to give you facts and how it was.
Solicitor	So, you asked more than one time for medication, that's what you mean?
JA	Yes, that would be better.
DC Bosomworth	Right.
JA	Yes, thank you.
DC Bosomworth	Yeah, but again I hadn't used the word 'begged', I'm afraid.
JA	No, I did.
DC Bosomworth	OK.
JA	No, I'm saying I used it too many times, didn't I?
DC Bosomworth	Yeah, what medication would that be then?
JA	There was a whole series of medication he went through. It was his idea. He was trying to get well. He had ideas. They didn't. So, we suggested. We said, we know you can't cure this terrible illness. We don't know what we're dealing with. This virus. Can we try this? This was him, not me. He was saying this.
DC Bosomworth	Right.
JA	I would go with him to the GP's surgery and sit and listen to him talk. He'd ask for all kinds of different medication used for rheumatoid arthritis, MS, anything he could think of to get well, but the reverse happened.

Perhaps a good place to begin is with the undisputed facts. Paul Anderson died on 18th July 2003. At the time of his death he was aged forty-three. He died of morphine poisoning. A post mortem

examination revealed no evidence of any natural disease causing or
contributing to his death. He had no physical condition and his mus-
culoskeletal system was normal.

Had medical assistance been summoned at the time the defendant
was told by Paul Anderson that he had taken enough this time, his
life would have been saved. Death only became inevitable in the short
period of time before Paul Anderson stopped breathing.

A simple act would have saved his life.

She should have called an ambulance.

From the Prosecution's closing speech

Tape 7: 25 January 2004: 14.51–15.24

DC Bosomworth	According to PC Boulton, you told her you returned about 1800 hours and I said I wasn't bothered whether it was 1800 or 1830. But you said to her, 'I thought he'd taken enough this time.' Do you recall saying that to her?
JA	No, because this is what happened. I went upstairs. Paul was waiting for me on the side of the bed. He said, 'I'm sorry, I can't stand the pain, I have taken enough this time,' and then he collapsed on the bed. So those words belong to him, not to me.
DC Bosomworth	Right and what do you think Paul meant by that, then?
JA	I have taken enough this time. I went numb and in shock. I didn't take responsibility. I walked halfway to the tablets to see what he'd taken. I walked back and I was hoping

he hadn't taken enough. Just let him sleep it
off and then he'd wake up and we'd carry
on.

DC Bosomworth Did you think he'd taken tablets then or not?

JA   I didn't take responsibility. I walked halfway
to the cabinet to look.

DC Bosomworth And did you think he'd taken tablets for
suicide?

JA   You never think it's going to happen. You've
been through it so many times. You've called
twice the ambulance, twice before. You've
fought in the garage over a hosepipe. You've
fought for his life for years.

DC Bosomworth Did it not cross your mind that he was
attempting suicide or had attempted suicide?

JA   You just don't believe it's going to happen
and I don't know. I can't tell you. I went
numb with shock that day. I couldn't lift the
phone. I'm sorry. I didn't call the ambulance.
I'd called twice before. He went immediately
to sleep.

DC Bosomworth So, did he go to sleep or did he lose consciousness?

JA   I wouldn't be able to tell you whether it was
sleep or consciousness.

DC Bosomworth But wouldn't that in itself give you alarm
bells in that he basically blurted the words
out, 'I've taken enough this time' and then
he'd have gone to sleep? Because he certainly
hasn't been conscious.

JA   He went into a deep sleep.

DC Bosomworth But wouldn't that raise alarm bells to you?

JA   I should have called the ambulance. I'm sorry. He said, 'I'm sorry.' I'm sorry too. We're both sorry.

In our courts, in almost every trial, there is a crime which involves an element of dishonesty or lust or violence; where someone has stolen property, raped someone, committed some terrible assault. This trial is almost unique because it involves a defendant who does not have an intention that is said to be dishonest or sexual or violent. It is about a defendant who behaves with love, understanding and consideration for someone who was racked with unremitting, constant pain . . .

We submit that what she did accounts to no crime at all.

From the Defence's closing speech

Tape 7: 25 January 2004: 14.51–15.24 continued

DC Bosomworth I wasn't going down this road at the moment, but it's fair to say that Paul had had enough.

JA   Every day we talked about recovery and him getting better. Every single day. We never discussed suicide. He'd make attempts and I'd forgive him. I didn't want him to die. I wanted him to be alive. I wanted to be ninety years old with him.

DC Bosomworth So why did you not ring the ambulance, then?

JA   I'm sorry. I didn't take responsibility.

DC Bosomworth In the second interview you said you'd been saving his life all weekend. What did you mean by that?

JA	He was suicidal and I tried to save his life all weekend. We talked about the future. We didn't talk about suicide. There was no assistance. I was trying to save his life.
DC Bosomworth	Let me just clarify that then, Jill. You said there was no assistance, so had Paul himself been talking about taking his own life that weekend?
JA	I was very worried about him, you know, I was ...
DC Bosomworth	You were very worried about him as regards ...
JA	His ... how he was feeling and the pain he was in.
DC Bosomworth	So had he discussed suicide that weekend?
JA	I wouldn't say he had discussed suicide. I said, 'Please stay alive.' There's a difference between that.
DC Bosomworth	So?
JA	I said to him ... All I can remember about that weekend is, I told him I would walk to the moon for him.
DC Bosomworth	So?
JA	I'd do anything for him, to keep him alive.
DC Bosomworth	Had he himself mentioned suicide to you that weekend?
JA	I don't ... He probably had, yes. I don't know.
DC Bosomworth	OK, had there been any other attempts that weekend?
JA	No.
DC Bosomworth	I'll just go back to the doctor, the Internet

and drug prescriptions. What medication did
you actually get off the Internet for Paul?

JA   Some friends sent some herbal remedies for
sleeping from the States that I'd possibly
found on the Internet.

DC Bosomworth   So you didn't actually purchase anything off
the Internet, then?

JA   I think I purchased an orthopaedic pillow for
him, but it was useless.

DC Bosomworth   It's fair to say, then, you weren't purchasing
drugs for him off the Internet?

JA   No.

DC Bosomworth   Medication?

JA   No, everything was via the GPs or the consultants.

DC Bosomworth   OK. Did you have any influence on what
drug prescriptions were given to Paul? Did
you ask the doctor for things, or did you
pester the doctor?

JA   Paul was running it. I did what he said.

DC Bosomworth   All right then. Did you pester the GP?

JA   Pester?

DC Bosomworth   On Paul's behalf because Paul wanted something.

JA   I would ask.

DC Bosomworth   Right.

JA   They might say I was pestering but I don't
care because I was trying to keep him alive.
I was trying to eliminate pain. So if I was a
pest, I'm happy to be one.

DC Bosomworth   Jill, no, I'm trying not to use the word 'beg'.

JA   Yes, I appreciate that, I'm sorry.

DC Bosomworth	I used the word 'pester'. I'm not saying you were a pest. Did you have to ask, on several occasions, for a certain prescription that Paul wanted?
JA	Yes, probably the GP's, they were trying to do their best. We were trying to do our best. The NHS is under-resourced and over-stretched. We'd hit heads together over the illness, of course, because everybody else does. They're trying to understand. What are they supposed to do? It's enormously frustrating for doctors to see a person like Paul.
DC Richardson	Was there anything his GP prescribed that you would think he was reluctant to pre-scribe, except for your or Paul's insistence?
JA	Not that I'm aware of. We tried to do everything professionally and he was in crippling pain. They didn't have any sug-gestions so we tried to suggest things ourselves.

May 1997

He held the magnifying glass close to his eyes and peered at the mushroom. It was slimy with a brown top and white root. He checked his fungi book again and turned to me.

'Scaly wood mushroom, *agaricus langei*, or maybe we'll find *abortiporus biennis*, blushing rosette.' He winked. 'Or perhaps a puffball.'

'Mmm, sounds lovely,' I said.

I stood by him as he examined the mushroom. He rolled it

around in his hand and held it up to the light. He reached into the pocket of his all-weather jacket and brought out a sandwich bag into which he placed the specimen along with the others he had already collected. Then he moved on to the next clump of mushrooms.

We had arrived at the woods around noon. It was a short drive from Rose Cottage along the Pateley Bridge–Ripon road. It was a balmy spring day; primroses and bluebells edged the paths and lay at the foot of the trees, oak, beech and birch. Birdsong filled the air. Sunlight struggled to pierce the canopy of green above our heads. He came to a shaft of light. Vitamin D from sunlight, would that cure him? He stood with his face lifted to a weak sun, as clouds broke through the rays.

He seemed to know what he was looking for. He kept putting mushrooms in his sandwich bag. We came upon a clump of white mushrooms. He examined them carefully and after some moments turned to me and said, '*Amanita verna*, the destroying angel, related to the death cap. Don't ever eat them – they're deadly poisonous.' He peered at me and his glasses slipped down his nose.

He picked some wild flowers, giving me most of their names and squinting at the ones he did not know. We carried on walking, maybe 8 or 9 miles that day. We passed a cottage surrounded by peacocks. We were admiring them when a woman came out and asked us what we were doing. 'Admiring your peacocks,' we said. She gave us a 'local look', which meant, 'Get lost'. We had got used to that look. This was a place where the locals wanted it all to themselves, and even though tourism was a key source of income, tourists were welcome only in the sections allocated to them by the indigenous population. These sections comprised the high streets, where the merchandise was displayed, and local attractions with entrance fees.

Finally, we had to turn homeward. When the day was gone, I walked round our home admiring the jam jars filled with wildflowers. I went upstairs to see him and he was propped up in bed immersed in his wild flower book. He had wild flowers spread out on the duvet around him and a magnifying glass. He was in deep concentration. I left him. When I went into the kitchen, the oven was on. There was a strange smell. I opened the oven door and, in neat rows, there were mushrooms baking.

Tape 7: 25 January 2004: 14.51–15.24 continued

DC Richardson	Right, Jill, just going on to a different part of the interview now. Your house was searched?
JA	Yes.
DC Richardson	When you came in to speak to us last time, various articles had been recovered. We've had a chance to look through them and hopefully you'll recognize them, so I'll just ask you some questions. It's about your journals in which you wrote your everyday thoughts, basically like a diary entry.
JA	It's therapy. It never goes anywhere.
DC Richardson	Right, OK. So that is some way ...
JA	It's a classic way to cope.
DC Richardson	... of dealing with it?
JA	Yes. It was my anger and frustration, which is normal as a carer.
DC Richardson	That's fine.
JA	You can talk to any carer in this country, six million of them. I was told to write down my

feelings by the ME Association and I'm also a creative writer. You will find some very interesting things among my effects. You went into one of the drawers that no one was ever supposed to go into. I appreciate you are doing an investigation. I appreciate it was a death at home. I respect that, but Paul never went into that drawer, and no one was ever supposed to see that drawer, so you're going to see some very interesting things. I was frustrated and angry and the way I dealt with it was to write it down.

DC Richardson	We're not . . .
JA	I'm not here to hurt people.
DC Richardson	We're only going to present you here with what we think may be relevant, i.e. we don't . . . We will try and respect your privacy as much as we can and that's what we'll continue doing.
JA	Well, you'll see things that no one was supposed to see, not even my husband . . .
DC Richardson	We're professionals as well.
JA	Of course.
JA	This was just my way of getting out my anger and frustration.
DC Richardson	How did Isla give you the job of caring for Paul?
JA	She came to visit us with the family and she looked into my eyes and said, 'Take care of my boy for me,' and she said that when she was in hospital, just before she died, 'Please take care of my boy.'

DC Richardson	And how did you interpret that?
JA	I became his carer. I didn't plan to be his carer. We had a normal marriage like everybody else. As everyone knows the world is not geared to easy; things happen and plans change and there are lots of people who are caring for their married partners.
DC Richardson	We've discussed the problems in the family. You actually said the word 'bullying'.
JA	Yes.
DC Richardson	What do you mean by bullying?
JA	My family have had difficulty understanding Chronic Fatigue Syndrome. They said Paul should be out of bed and getting to work, which I understand.
DC Richardson	I'm assuming there you're referring to your mother?
JA	Yes, probably, she wants the best for her daughter.
DC Richardson	But she said something like, 'Paul, get up, get out of bed and get to work.'
JA	No, not like that.
DC Richardson	I've quoted what you said now . . .
JA	I've used the wrong words. She couldn't understand the illness and why he wasn't out of bed.
DC Richardson	Were there any other members of your family that you had problems with as well?
JA	Yes, they're very 'old school' in mentality. I appreciate that they say things that they now realize are not helpful, but I understand also why they said those things. We were frustrated

too. You have to remember that we wanted to be part of the family. We wanted to be with my family having a cup of tea. I'd be talking to my mother and Paul would be fixing electrics. All this was taken off us, so there was frustration on both sides but they hung in and they kept on going with us. You have to remember you do take a lot of frustration and anger out on your nearest and dearest, so you will find things, nasty things. I've said things about my family that were never supposed to go anywhere else except for my 'anger drawer' because the ME Association told me to do that.

DC Richardson   ALG46A. It was an envelope containing those things there . . .

JA   Yes, I've those . . .

DC Richardson   Can you remember that? Obviously, it was found in your house, therefore it was never sent.

JA   Yes.

DC Richardson   Was it intended to be sent?

JA   No, never. None of this stuff. It's my drawer. No one on the planet was supposed to see it, not even Paul.

DC Richardson   OK. I'm showing an envelope stuffed with similar sorts of paper addressed to his father.

JA   I just write them now and again when I'd think about them. They'd call up and we'd have these very aggressive conversations with them, bu Paul did not say those things. He was lovely.

May 1994

We were surrounded by butterflies. We were in the butterfly house in Syon Park on the outskirts of London. The heat enveloped our skins; steam rose from somewhere. The butterflies were all shades of the rainbow. Tropical plants – spiky palms, olive bamboos, lush green ferns, orchids in white, pink, purple, blue – sprouted from the sides of the walkway as we moved through amid a crowd of people. It was a cold, rainy Saturday, yet, inside this covered enclosure, we could have been deep in the jungles of South America.

A large butterfly, with exquisitely etched markings in black and white, alighted before us on a pink orchid. It extended its proboscis and dug it deep into the orchid for a long drink. We watched with everyone else, fascinated. There were moths, too. Somehow, they were more aggressive and less agreeable than the butterflies, but equally fascinating. We stayed for a long time and walked through several times from beginning to end. All the patterns imaginable fluttered around us. A butterfly landed on Paul's shoulder. We watched as it settled, searching for food. It was large and orange with a delicate white pattern on its wings. Afterwards we visited a café and held hands as we ordered cakes and tea. The butterflies had given us a feeling of peace and fragility.

Tape 7: 25 January 2004: 14.51–15.24 continued

DC Richardson	In there it mentions something about Paul being mistreated by his father. What did you mean by that?
JA	We'd had this telephone conversation with

his father again. He was just so angry all the time. I think the reason was his grief for Isla. He said to me, 'If Paul tells you I hit him when he was a boy or child, I didn't, he's lying.' So I told Paul about that and Paul said, 'He did hit me.' Which is standard father-son relationship, but it was just the fact that he said that he'd never hit Paul. I don't know why he said that. It came out of the blue in this telephone conversation, just out of the blue. It wasn't initiated by me.

DC Richardson	So would it be fair to say that this is how you were feeling at the time?
JA	I have my moments of frustration and anger. I just put it down on paper.
DC Richardson	Did it help?
JA	It absolutely helps, yes ...
DC Richardson	So how did you feel after you'd done this?
JA	I felt better because I'd actually expressed what I'd like to say, but would never say.
DC Richardson	But you obviously did treat the people who disagreed with you with a lot of contempt. We'll carry on with what I'm showing you. Because they disagreed with what you and Paul believed.
JA	Contempt ... they initiated the contempt, didn't they? We set off with very good relationships with them and they just deteriorated over time, like his body, in a way. I can't give you an explanation. Contempt, I hate, I don't like that word. I was just angry with them.

DC Richardson	OK, who's the . . .
JA	Because they disagreed, but it wasn't the disagreement, it was the fact they were aggressive. I mean, I don't know how you'd feel if your brother called you up and said he wanted to kill you.
DC Richardson	Oh, he's done it many times.
JA	Right.
DC Richardson	Who is 'Doctor W'? I'd just remind you that this is also from the red book.
JA	Oh dear, I can't even remember which doctor that would be.
DC Richardson	Is it somebody who disagreed with you or that you came up against?
JA	It was just a very difficult illness to deal with. It was awful seeing my husband physically disintegrate.

September 1993

The silver cars with purple and yellow lights whirled round. We gripped the sides until we were giddy. A lean, tall man ran between us, pushing the cars if they came too close together as they span. It looked like his life was at risk, but he was nimble. The purple, red and orange lights dazzled us, bouncing off the silver steel floor. We were on the dodgems. People were screaming with fear and laughter. We joined them.

The cars suddenly came to a halt with one push of a button. We looked at each other and the many flushed, merry faces around us. We slid out of the car and strolled around the many amusement sideshows. We arrived at a stall with guns on strings, which, for a few coins, you could aim at ducks floating along a makeshift river. Paul had a go. He tried a few shots and then looked at the barrel of the gun.

'They've fixed it,' he said.

'Can't have many winners,' I said.

He persisted until, at last, he had managed to hit the ducks three times. The man running the stall looked bemused.

'Pick a prize,' he said, pointing to a selection of fluffy toys.

Paul looked at me. 'I did it for you.'

'I'll have that one,' I said, choosing a small, fluffy white teddy bear with blue eyes and a blue striped waistcoat.

The man looked at me. 'Let me guess where you're from,' he said. He had the weather-beaten face of the road traveller, a member of the tight-knit community of funfair people. 'I've been all over the country and I can always recognize an accent,' he said. He was quiet for a moment. 'Sheffield.'

'You're absolutely right.' I was taken aback. Not many people recognized my accent.

The man grinned at me, handing over my teddy bear. 'Farewell,' he said.

We moved on. We spotted the ghost train ride, and in moments we were in a buggy on a track as it set off into a gloomy tunnel full of ghosts, ghouls and Draculas who leered out at us. People screamed and I hid my face on Paul's arm. The ride came to an end and we tumbled out. We strolled towards the exit and onto the road. I held the teddy bear to my face and then to Paul's.

'What shall we call him?' I asked.

'Humbug,' he said.

'No that's . . . how about Pierre?' I suggested.

'He's not French.'

We looked around. A van sped past us with 'Martin's Scaffolding' on the side.

Paul turned to me. 'Mart.'

I nodded and gave the bear to Paul, who tucked him under his arm. The three of us walked on.

Tape 7: 25 January 2004: 14.51–15.24 continued

DC Richardson	Do you recall then what made you angry with Doctor W?
JA	No, I think one doctor told him to go away and take an aspirin. I'm not very proud of my behaviour but this is all very private and no one ever knew about it. When I dealt with his family I tried to be pleasant and kind to them.
DC Richardson	You referred there to repressed homosexuals and somebody with emotional problems.
JA	Mm.
DC Richardson	Was that part of your feeling of the problem or was that you getting anger out?
JA	It was just me being nasty.
DC Richardson	Right. It mentions there that 'real' men do not pick on women. Can you explain that?
JA	Yes, because the landlord was harassing me.
Solicitor	I'm getting a bit concerned about this because this lady's been here since 10.30 this morning. She's now being invited to look at a large number of documents and she's clearly struggling. I'm going to suggest that we terminate this interview.
DC Richardson	And do what?
Solicitor	And have a break, a significant break, because she's been here for five hours.

DC Richardson	That's . . . that's fine, no problem at all.
Solicitor	I think.
DC Richardson	I did mention in disclosure.
Solicitor	Yeah.
DC Richardson	We were planning on doing and if you had problems there . . .
Solicitor	I know but I didn't realize there were so many documents.
DC Richardson	I did mention that . . .
Solicitor	But you didn't tell me how many . . .
DC Bosomworth	We did offer a meal.
Solicitor	Well, the meal's not the issue. The issue is that she's been here since 10.30 a.m. She's been subject to intense questioning. This is now the fourth interview and there are a number of documents here you are asking her to comment on and she's entitled to a significant break and I think she needs one.
DC Richardson	No problem at all. We can certainly stop here.
Solicitor	She needs it.

Tape 8: 26 January 2004: 9.54–10.37

DC Richardson	OK, first of all, thank you very much for the consents, medical consents and the financial consents, which you gave us prior to the interview. What I want to do now is to continue where we left off yesterday. Let me just jog your memory. I was referring to some writing from a red book that I've underlined just briefly that says 'real men

	do not pick on women'. Can you explain that to me?
JA	I don't remember writing it, but obviously I wanted to pour out feelings.
DC Richardson	It looks like some of it was obviously used later when you did your tribute, that you had similar sorts of words and everything.
JA	I'm sure it was. The tribute was just for personal friends, no one else.
DC Richardson	But when was this written?
JA	I couldn't tell you.
DC Richardson	I just want to refresh my own memory. I've mentioned some reference there to Isla. Could you explain to me what that means? In what context that was?
JA	It's just, Isla and Paul's philosophy was to go out and make people laugh and that's how he felt about life.

June 1997

One day at Rose Cottage he called me to bed. The bedroom was small with a thick, acrylic, sky blue carpet and wallpaper with rosebuds dotted all over a white background. Our bed fitted snugly between the two white bedside cabinets. A television and VCR stood on top of a bookshelf. His side of the bed was close to a small, crooked window. It was dangerous. The frame was old and rotting and the glass in it looked as if it might fall out. The cottage was at the centre of a little village, population ninety-seven. Rose Cottage had been part of a large house that had been divided into two. It was called a cottage because it looked like one, whether it was or not. It was constructed of grey

Yorkshire stone and had seen almost a century. Some people would call it 'nothing very much', but location is everything. The village should have been a place where health has the best opportunity to return.

Because it was called Rose Cottage, we had planted a rose at the front door called Lady Hillingdon. She crept slowly up and around the door, but we would leave before she had time to make real roots and take off. There was another rose too, a wild white one. We did not know the name. It was old and had been attached to the front wall of the cottage for many years. It flowered abundantly in June, and after its initial bloom the small lawn in front of the cottage was covered in a confetti of rose petals.

When he called me to bed that night, it was the end of another day of hard graft. As I came up to the bedroom door, it moved. When I entered the room, a picture shifted on the wall. The light was off and there was a muggy, grey half-light from outside that seemed to put the bedroom into shade. As I approached a cabinet, an ornament moved. Then there was outrageous laughter. He had attached a piece of white cotton thread to all of these objects. It was wrapped around the bedroom door handle and he was manipulating everything from under the bed covers like a puppeteer. The cotton thread was wound around his fingers and feet. He had a thing for ghosts and anything to do with other worlds.

He had always been a prankster. I remember stories members of his family had told me. So his time incarcerated in this room provided opportunity for entertainment late at night when work was done. These were the days when he was forced to spend half of the week lying in bed. So pranks were a welcome distraction.

On another occasion, I had jumped into bed beside him only

to get out again quickly. A large black beetle greeted me. He had made it from paper and a black marker. It was detailed. A beetle with six legs. I picked it up to examine it and it had a set of white, sharp teeth which grinned back at me.

Tape 8: 26 January 2004: 9.54–10.37 continued

DC Richardson   There's mention of harassment as well. You may have covered this, but is that the same harassment that you're talking about from the farmer?

JA   No. I was an angry, frustrated woman when I was writing those things because I was seeing my husband ill and bedridden. I couldn't stop his decline so I said all these things at the time and they're just very personal.

DC Richardson   You've mentioned the families being a disgrace but why were you saying that? What was going through your mind to say that?

JA   It was the frustration that Paul was losing his health. He could not achieve what he wanted to achieve in life. I was jealous. I mean my husband wanted to support me and give me a fantastic life. He wanted to make money and it was all denied him because of his health problems.

DC Richardson   Is this aimed at your mother because she'd done something or said something or . . . ?

JA   Oh, it was a mother and daughter relationship. We were always having spats.

DC Richardson	Right, and what was this in relation to? What really wound you up to make you write that?
JA	Oh, I've no idea.
DC Richardson	OK.
JA	It's a mother-daughter. She took the brunt of the illness and I was horrible to her.
DC Richardson	Right.
JA	And I've apologized and I regret how I felt. I was an angry woman. I could not make my husband better. He couldn't make himself better. He tried everything. And I'd go out and I'd meet her in Harrogate. We'd have this big argument about nothing. I'd come back and Paul would counsel me again, 'Your mother loves you, just ignore it, she doesn't mean it.'
DC Richardson	Was it in relation to Paul's illness?
JA	Oh, we've been at it for forty-eight years. Obviously she was concerned and worried for me and for Paul.
DC Richardson	Right.
JA	She would ask about our money situation and I wanted to say to her everything's fine and it wasn't. It's just things like that.
DC Richardson	Right.
JA	And it's just a mother loving her daughter and I didn't do it as well as I should have done. I'm the first to admit that and Paul would verify that if he was here.
DC Richardson	The next one.
JA	He supported her all the way. Paul and I loved each other and we just tried to do our best and that's it.

DC Richardson	Obviously, you were supporting Paul against his family in respect.
JA	It was his decision. I was his wife. He came first.
DC Richardson	Is there any suggestion then of you using Paul as a weapon against his family?
JA	No, not at all, I would never do that. I hoped and prayed for him that they would come to us with apologies. I know they've written letters. He read his sister's letter. It was his decision. He said he could not cope. He was too ill to cope with petty arguments and I said I'm too busy taking care of you and that was his decision.

This was unremitting pain for him and, you may think, unremitting sacrifice for her. It was she who cooked; she who cleaned; she who drove; she who shopped; she who changed the beds; she who wrote the letters. What a joyless existence, coupled with the fact that she lives with a man who cannot support her anymore, cannot protect her. You may think, if she had taken an overdose with a fixed intention to die, you might not have been surprised if she had found it all too much.

From the Defence's closing speech

Tape 8: 26 January 2004: 9.54–10.37 continued

| JA | He made all the decisions about his family and I made the decisions about my family. He told me at the beginning of the relationship, and I love him all the more for that; he said |

he would never interfere in my family relationships or any of my friendships. Bless
him. He never ever did.

DC Richardson   Was Paul aware of these writings that I've
shown you today and yesterday?

JA   No. He was wonderful. He let me let off
steam and it was private. He never inter-
fered. I had my private drawer. I had my
books and he never even looked. I remember
once he found a little tiny scrap of paper in
the office. He picked it up and looked at it
briefly and then handed it to me without a
word.

DC Richardson   And that was something similar to what I've
been showing you?

JA   He understood. I wrote everything in there
and it never went anywhere to anyone.

DC Richardson   So it was never sent out to anyone at all?

JA   No, I mean, there are some letters that
did go to his GP. You've got those in the
file and they are professional letters. These
are not professional letters, they're just
me letting off for my own personal way of
coping. I was just getting carried away with
my imagination. How I wanted the world to
respond to Paul's Chronic Fatigue Syndrome
and it's not yet recognized, as you know
probably from your own research. It was
me imagining how wonderful it would be
if all the doctors signed this letter. It's
irrelevant. It doesn't mean anything, it's
just me.

DC Richardson	Your thoughts.
JA	My thoughts and my way of coping with . . .
DC Richardson	I'm not saying it's anything different. I just wanted to try and understand what you're going through.
JA	Of course, yes I understand. I appreciate that.
DC Richardson	Is this then, trying to put it right in my mind, some kind of Utopian idea?
JA	Yes.
DC Richardson	That you would like his GP and the consultant's viewpoint on ME?
JA	I suppose so, but they're just names. They could be any doctor.
DC Richardson	Right, medical professional then?
JA	Yes, I mean, some of this is history because it is now starting to get more recognition. To some extent, Paul was vindicated because a lot of what he said about his physical symptoms were getting more and more documented and accepted by the medical profession. They don't know what to do. They did their best and it's all a learning process for everybody.
DC Richardson	Let me just show you ALG43. It's a similar type of letter. This one appears to be dated in a similar way to the first letter.
JA	It's irrelevant, it's just me.
DC Richardson	It . . . appears to be written in September. One's October. It's a similar sort of thing.
JA	Yes. It's just me letting rip or letting off steam. It never went anywhere, it's just . . .

DC Richardson	The difference is, this time it's also got Paul's GP's name at the bottom.
JA	Yes.
DC Richardson	But it's also got yours and Paul's name at the bottom.
JA	It's just fantasy. I had the common sense not to show these to anyone.
DC Richardson	OK.
JA	It was just the feelings that I was going through at the time.
DC Richardson	Why the reference to respect?
JA	I think 'respect' is a word we all use, isn't it? It's just a word.
DC Richardson	But the letter is used in a particular context. That's what I'm trying to get the meaning of.
JA	It's just ...
DC Richardson	What made you say or write 'respect' in there?
JA	I suppose, because I think respect means people who listen to others. I think any carer, every carer, should consider themselves heroes, that's my philosophy. I have met so many people who are carers and I would like in the future to do things with carers' organizations.
DC Richardson	ALG44. Similar sort of writing. It's a letter to the families.
JA	Yes, that's me letting rip at the families, because if you've gone on a Chronic Fatigue Syndrome website you can see that this particular sort of illness is causing horrendous problems between families. You cannot fulfil

your family duties. All we wanted to do was go and visit them. We couldn't do any of that. As you know it's been a rough ride and I just let rip and it's just a load of rubbish again.

DC Richardson	You've made reference.
JA	I never sent this to anyone.
DC Richardson	I appreciate that but this is how you were feeling?
JA	It's just feelings, but if I showed this, to a psychiatrist or a counsellor, they'd say, 'Oh you're completely normal, Jill.' It was just feelings and emotions. Ultimately it was about me feeling powerless.
DC Richardson	This is a more angry letter, isn't it, at this point? This is reference to murdering women and things like that.
JA	Probably during the time when the Taliban were on the TV. They took a woman out into the football pitch and shot her in the head. I probably watched that and got really angry and put this on paper.
DC Richardson	So it's a mix of what you see happening in the world and your feelings?
JA	Yes.
DC Richardson	Is that fair to say?
JA	Yes, I mean, we were in the cottage and I made the decision to stay with him. I didn't like leaving him on his own. He was very frail, so the media was a big source, a big part of our lives. It had to be. We tried to use all of our time productively. He used his time

positively. He was a positive thinker. As you can tell, I'm far more negative. I wish I wasn't, but I think possibly carers get angrier than the actual patient. As a patient he was a joy and a pleasure. He was a brilliant patient.

DC Richardson   This is DE1. This is written as though it's a bit different to perhaps your previous letters which put your feelings down on paper. It looks like a draft of a letter to someone. You've entitled it there, 'Dearest One, my True and Good Friend'. Who was that addressed to?

JA   That is one of my friends, Vanessa. She died just before Christmas. She was fifty-three. She had cancer. Both her parents were Auschwitz survivors.

DC Richardson   There are obvious references there to part of your life and the part that we're interested in is where you've had the fall-out with the family.

JA   When Isla was alive I thought they were the most fantastic people. I told them that, so a few things got out and about and they've taken the hump. I wish they hadn't but they misinterpreted me and I can't do anything about that.

DC Richardson   There's a reference here to right wing and Nazis. Is that how you view Paul's family or people who disagree with you?

JA   No, it's just me mouthing off. It doesn't mean anything. Perhaps I'd watched that series. I don't know whether you saw it on

	Channel Five. It was an excellent programme on Hitler and the people who worked for him. We all do our thing, don't we, and have a bit of a mouth-off about this, that and the other, and that's just mine.
DC Richardson	It mentions Paul's disappearing health and financial humiliation was being enjoyed. Did you believe that?
JA	I think his mother said to me there's a German word, *schadenfreude* – enjoyment of others' misfortunes. I think we all know, to be honest, that there is a certain amount of pleasure sometimes. That's human nature for seeing people fall flat on their faces. It's just the way human beings are.
DC Richardson	Did you believe that, though?
JA	Not really. It's a tough call when all your dreams get shattered but we did a first-class bankruptcy. No one got hurt. It was professional, the official receiver told him that. We made sure that no individual got hurt and we didn't want to go through it but it happened.
DC Richardson	There's reference to glory and struggle.
JA	Pilgrim's progress.
DC Richardson	And what do you mean by that? What were you referring to there?
JA	It's just the human story, isn't it? A big giant struggle for most people.
DC Richardson	Is that referring to Paul's illness or is that in general?
JA	Both. Whatever. It's just the way it is.

February 1994

It was a bitterly cold morning. He looked out of the window from our home, a studio flat on the seventh floor of a block in south-west London. A thick, solid, suffocating blanket of cloud clamped the city. He was getting ready for his work as a motorbike courier. It was pay-as-you-go. He knew the short cuts around town. He braced himself. He had rebuilt his motorbike, a secondhand Kawasaki. He had put down an old sheet on the floor of the lounge, stripped the engine and rebuilt it. He painted the engine phone-box red. He knew this activity annoyed me. I had to trip over engine parts, paint stripper and tools to get to the kitchen.

He put on several sweaters, a thick waterproof jacket and waterproof trousers. He wrapped newspapers around his feet and slipped them into his boots. This was a habit from childhood. He was used to being cold as a child. His family had often run out of money for the electricity meter and even their basic needs. He was nimble on a bike, probably as a result of his small, agile frame. We gave each other a peck on the cheek and parted. He went through the door with his helmet under his arm. I went off to work as usual.

I was doing a nine-to-five as an administrator at a local college. I was usually back home before him. Tonight I waited for him, anxious. I did not like his job. I wished for change. His previous job had been selling advertising space for a publishing company, but a recession hit. At last he arrived; we hugged and I got a chest of soot. He looked like a miner, with the whites of his eyes peering out at me from his grime-covered face. I ran a bath for him and he climbed into the tub.

It was Friday night and we wanted to go out. Sometimes we stayed in with a video and an Indian takeaway, but tonight we wanted to go into town. We liked to dress up on a Friday. He washed his hair and shaved again. He put on his cologne and checked his fingernails. He put on some smart khaki trousers, an ironed shirt, a sweater, brown leather shoes and a long, grey woollen coat, with his silk cravat. It was a rich burgundy with a navy motif. He only had one cravat and it was his favourite item.

I dressed for fun. He liked my legs, so I showed them off and wore a short red skirt, tight top, stockings and high heels. I put on more make-up than I usually wore during the day. He liked that and would say, 'Put some slap on.' He liked to see me with bright red lips and dark shaded eyes. It turned him on. We were average looking, not head-turners. He was slight with red-brown hair, and blue-green eyes. His face was sensitive. He had a small nose and a wry smile. His hair stood on end because he cut it himself and it ended up in a sort of hedgehog style. I had brown-red hair, too, and we shared the same coloured eyes. We both stooped slightly, due to hours hunched over computers or reading too much as kids. We shared a passion for information, any information, even stupid information. Doing this, getting dressed-up and going out together, made us feel cool and dreamy.

Friday night could be anywhere in the city, but his favourite place was a pub called The Swan in Bayswater. He often went on his own for a night out with the boys. But tonight I would accompany him. Sometimes I drove; sometimes he did. Tonight, it was my turn, but we never fought over it: driving was never an issue. But if I drove he would give instructions to me in a constant stream of barking commands: 'Use the wing mirrors, honk the horn more often so that other drivers know you're there, always watch the front, don't worry about the back, not too close, not too fast.' He tried to teach and I tried to learn. If we had an argument, it was usually in the car on a journey gone wrong or too slow or because some idiot was swerving about. He had a capacity for road rage. He noticed I was more pragmatic about the rules of the road. 'You need to be more assertive,' he would say to me. 'Your caution, the way you hesitate, confuses the other drivers.' I'd shrug and continue driving.

We arrived at The Swan and ordered our usual drinks at the bar. His friends had started to gather. Richard, an actor, and Graham, a solicitor, joined us regularly. We would often give Richard a lift home. There were others, too. Later we climbed up narrow, crooked wooden stairs at the back of the pub to a room at the top. Tonight it was packed with a group of about thirty Scandinavians. We took a seat next to an elderly Swedish couple and exchanged greetings. They all spoke English. We felt embraced by these blond, blue-eyed people from the icy northern regions. There was only one activity on everyone's mind and that was singing: 'Hello, Dolly!', 'Cabaret', 'Okalahoma', 'Downtown', 'New York, New York', 'Hey Jude' and some Nordic ones too, culminating in 'Auld Lang Syne'. By the time we went home, our faces were blush-red. There was laughter on tap.

Tape 8: 26 January 2004: 9.54–10.37 continued

DC Richardson	You also referred to boiling cauldrons of petty jealousies?
JA	Yes, jealousy's everywhere, isn't it?
DC Richardson	Yeah, but are you referring to anyone in particular, such as Paul's family?
JA	Probably, I'm just mouthing off again.

DC Richardson	Was there any jealousy?
JA	That's my honest feeling that a lot of his problems were jealousy of the relationship with Isla. There were three of us.
DC Richardson	Yes, sorry you did mention that.
JA	We were just so close and sometimes I can remember being up there in Scotland, when he was well enough, and the three of us couldn't stop talking. It was magnetic. I think there's jealousy everywhere, isn't there, and particularly among families. She was an amazing woman who loved all her children equally, but she just loved him that bit more.
DC Richardson	So this is something that you've surmised from actions, words, is that correct?
JA	He had a very unusual childhood. I don't know whether they talked to you about his childhood.
DC Richardson	We've seen obviously his medical records and there are references to his childhood as well.
JA	He left school at thirteen and educated himself. His mother was the one who allowed him to do that, which is quite a thing. It's what she told me. He told me that he just turned up to school, took the exams and the teachers asked him if he'd been on a nice holiday. He got good grades.
DC Richardson	He was able to learn.
JA	Self-taught.
DC Richardson	I'm not a psychologist. I'm not qualified to

say, but agree with me or disagree with me, in the last six months of Paul's life you were under an incredible strain and pressure. That stress and strain was showing in things you've written. Is that true?

JA   I was very worried about him. I was dedicated to his survival, that's all I wanted.

DC Richardson   OK, did you see a change in your character?

JA   I would certainly assess myself as under pressure at that time.

DC Bosomworth   Mike, you've got about three minutes left.

DC Richardson   OK, we'll just finish this off.

JA   Yes, but I was dedicated to his life.

DC Richardson   I appreciate that but it appears that things have changed a bit more now. You mentioned that word 'paranoia'. I wouldn't know how to define that but you're talking about a change of character here. You're misinterpreting the actions of others, which is, I would say, not the person that you were twelve months prior to that. Were you seeking any medical help? Did you recognize that your character was changing and did you do something about it at this point?

JA   The problem was I'd been getting up for eight years, taking care of him, and I'd just keep on getting up and doing it and you don't realize.

DC Richardson   Right. In hindsight, are you saying that there was a change in your character?

JA   I've got hindsight for the rest of my life.

DC Richardson   Do you see that?

JA	I know I was under pressure but it was all about saving his life.
DC Richardson	Did you have a breakdown?
JA	No, no one diagnosed me with a breakdown. I was just keeping very, very busy.
DC Richardson	Were you concerned for your mental well-being?
JA	I was just trying to do my best.
DC Richardson	OK, Jill.

Indeed, the doctor underlined to you 'He was in pain from whatever cause. This isn't imagined pain. Wherever it came from – his mind or his body – it was real pain.' And that is why morphine was prescribed.

The amount found in his body was of the level found where a person dies from morphine overdose. It was ten times the therapeutic value; the value that would do some good.

That Paul believed his illness, his pain, was physical, surely does not mean he is of unsound mind. He is entitled to his view.

From the Defence's closing speech

Tape 9: 26 January 2004: 10.58–11.16

DC Bosomworth	And you had spats with your mother?
JA	Oh yes, mother, daughter . . . just like most people. There were bits and pieces, things that were said from all sides and it's just the way families are.
DC Bosomworth	And did you naturally find, for want of better words, your mother's criticism easier to take rather than that of Paul's family?

JA	I think criticism's hard to take wherever it comes from and I don't deal with it as well as I should.
DC Bosomworth	But would you deal with it better from your mother, perhaps, than say Paul's family?
JA	Probably because my mother's a blood relation, you know. It's hard to take it on the chin, isn't it?
DC Bosomworth	My colleague's gone through an awful lot of notes that you wrote down at some point. I think it's fair to say it's part of your anger management, if you like.
JA	Yes.
DC Bosomworth	And do you feel better once they're written down?
JA	Absolutely, it's just therapy and it's for no one else, just me.
DC Bosomworth	So why keep 'em?
JA	God knows, I should have chucked all of them. I mean, I know that. I should have cleared that drawer out but it was on the 'to do' list.
DC Bosomworth	So there's no particular reason you kept them, then?
JA	None at all. It's just I always meant to sort that drawer out and I didn't get round to it.
DC Bosomworth	Right. You use the word 'counselling' regularly. I've noticed that in this last interview and also the previous interviews yesterday. What do you actually mean by that word; for instance, you said Paul would counsel you after an argument with your mum?

JA	Talking things over.
DC Bosomworth	So counselling is talking things over, is it?
JA	Yes and, as I said, he never interfered in my family relationships and he was supportive towards my mother.
DC Bosomworth	His sister mentioned when we spoke to her, that you twist things around and it's a phrase you've actually used yourself.
JA	Well, I'm sorry if I do that.
DC Bosomworth	Erm.
JA	I don't think so. I try to give facts and stick to the facts.
DC Bosomworth	I mean, has his sister got things right that you do twist things to suit yourself or twist things that have been said to put them in a different context, if you like?
JA	I wouldn't like to think so. I've always tried to be sympathetic towards people, listen to them, do the best that I can for them, be nice and kind to people. And that's how I was to her.
DC Bosomworth	And, I know it's going to be difficult, but could you estimate how much you've spent on Paul's health?
JA	Oh yes, I was spending about fifty pounds a month at Boots on over-the-counter.
DC Bosomworth	That's on over-the-counter medicines alone.
JA	Yes.
DC Bosomworth	And that's not taking into account then the private consultations and things like that?
JA	No.
DC Bosomworth	And what about prescriptions then, are they to pay for?

JA	In the last year we got one of those pre-paid prescriptions for him which was a big saving.
DC Bosomworth	Also when my colleague was going through your writings . . .
JA	Yes.
DC Bosomworth	You said if a psychiatrist saw it he would think you were normal. Now have we suggested you're not normal?
JA	Well, that's just my own personal comment, you know. Everyone's free to make their own judgement.
DC Bosomworth	Yeah, I wonder why you came out with the term 'normal'. Have you ever undergone psychiatric treatment?
JA	No, I went to see a psychiatrist once but that was just for a chit-chat in Pateley Bridge.
DC Bosomworth	Right. That would be on your medical record, I would assume.
JA	Yes, it will. I went to see Dr Marion Anderson and she was very helpful.
DC Bosomworth	You said Paul's family had taken the hump . . .
JA	Yes.
DC Bosomworth	Had you and Paul not also taken the hump with them?
JA	Yes, I'd agree with that statement because it was a break, a complete breakdown in communication.
DC Bosomworth	You said you tried to negotiate a compromise within the family. How?
JA	I talked to his father constantly, as I described, as soon as Isla died.

DC Bosomworth	Right. Did you at any time tell any member of the family they'd never see Paul again?
JA	No.
DC Bosomworth	When was the bankruptcy?
Solicitor	Can you just slow down a bit?
DC Bosomworth	Sorry.
Solicitor	I know you're ...
DC Bosomworth	Yeah.
Solicitor	I know you're firing these questions at the lady but it's very difficult for her and it's a very stressful situation. So I know we're anxious to get on with it but if you can take your time, please.
DC Bosomworth	When was the bankruptcy?
JA	1999.
DC Bosomworth	How do you know Paul left school at the age of thirteen?
JA	He told me.
DC Bosomworth	Paul and Isla were obviously very close?
JA	Extremely.
DC Bosomworth	And I think, you said, although not her favourite, she probably had a soft spot for Paul, although she loved all her children equally?
JA	She loved all her children equally.
DC Bosomworth	But she had a particular soft spot for Paul?
JA	She certainly did, yes.
DC Bosomworth	Since Isla died, do you think you took her place in Paul's life?
JA	I think it's interesting because I read an article somewhere that most people in most marriages you actually chose your father or

your mother to marry. I don't know whether you've ever come across that theory. I think I matched her. I have a very similar personality to Isla but I didn't replace her as his mother. I never mothered him. It was a man-woman relationship. It was a marriage.

DC Bosomworth Right.

March 1998

'What was that? A shooting star?'

'A comet, maybe,' he replied.

Something had flashed in the sky above us. It was just before midnight and we were standing in the garden at Rose Cottage. The night sky was crystal clear, out here away from the lights of the big cities. I took a deep breath of pure, fresh night air. I listened as he spoke. He had been reading a book he had bought about the cosmos. He pointed to the twinkling mass above us.

'That's the Plough.'

'Yeah.'

'And over there is the North Star, the brightest.'

I looked up and north. He was right. It shone out, brighter than the other stars.

'There's the Big Dipper.'

'Lovely.'

'And the Milky Way,' he said. He traced the pathway of stars with his arm. Above us the sky twinkled a million lights.

We walked further up the garden and shone our torches into the pond he had made. Several frogs and toads jumped into the water from their stone perches to escape the beams. We counted about seven regulars: small, medium and large. They all had a one-size-fits-all name – Divey. So we had Divey One, Divey

Two and so on. We had to check on them most nights. They were a family of sorts. The light in my torch dimmed. I shook it.

'Piece of junk. My battery's gone.' My torch went out and I stood closer to him to catch the beam from his. 'Do you think the neighbours think we're off our heads?' I said.

'Why would they notice?'

'Because that's what neighbours do.'

'So what, they're just as cooked as we are.' He shrugged.

We continued walking up the garden. My eyes had adjusted to the night. I knew all the paths and beds. We reached one of the beds where we had planted daffodils. They were past their best and shrivelling. I broke off some of the brown foliage and tossed it onto one of the compost heaps I had scattered at various locations. The tulips were shooting up now and the air was sweeter every day.

We came out of the garden and passed the terraced cottages that were our neighbours' homes. I looked to see if any of their lights were on. Nothing stirred. We came up the path to the front door of Rose Cottage and slipped off our wellington boots.

'I'm going to make a hot chocolate,' I said.

Paul went up the stairs to the bedroom without comment. I walked into the lounge. The fire was dying in the grate. Something moved on the rug. I moved closer. A large toad was sitting in front of the fire as if warming itself. I looked at it and it looked back at me. I had seen it before but it was usually resting on the front doorstep of Rose Cottage. It had slipped in. Somehow we must have left the front door slightly ajar, perhaps when we were looking for our torches and putting our boots on. I went to the bottom of the stairs.

'Paul, we've got a visitor.'

'What?'

He came down.

'Look.'

The toad took no notice of us and remained seated.

'Come on then, come on then,' he said. He scooped the amphibian up in his hands, took it to the front door and released it. It hopped away without a croak.

Tape 9: 26 January 2004: 10.58–11.16 continued

JA	And there was never any mothering of him. He was his own man and made his own decisions. He made most of the decisions in our marriage. We discussed everything, but he was the leader.
DC Bosomworth	You used the phrase, 'It's all about saving his life.' Was that your care for him?
JA	Yes, I loved him. I wanted him to live. I wanted him to recover.
DC Bosomworth	So people actually die from Chronic Fatigue Syndrome itself?
JA	Every dream and hope I had was for Paul's recovery from that illness because other people were making it.
DC Bosomworth	Right, I've no more questions now.
JA	But I'll say this. He got a really bad case and his immune system was compromised at birth, as you know. Then, when he got this virus, it was the end of him.
DC Richardson	Jill, obviously you know an awful lot about the illness. You've done an awful lot of research on the Internet.
JA	Yes.

DC Richardson	Probably with Paul's leadership, is that correct?
JA	Yes. But it was on his behalf.
DC Richardson	Yeah, and you discovered quite a lot and probably more so than a lot of doctors who are not specializing.
JA	Yes.
DC Richardson	You mentioned that people don't necessarily die of this.
JA	No.
DC Richardson	But their life, I would assume, from Paul's experience, becomes intolerable.
JA	It radically alters, but Paul got a very bad case because he had a compromised immune system and then he got all this bone business on top.
DC Richardson	Right.
JA	For most people it's bad but not as bad.
DC Richardson	I don't know whether we've ever said this, but Paul obviously committed suicide.
JA	Yes.
DC Richardson	Did he do that because of the pain that he was in?
JA	Yes.
Solicitor	Well, do you know that, Mrs Anderson?
JA	No, I don't. It was on his suicide note because he was in terrible pain.
DC Richardson	How many people know then, following Paul's sad death, that he committed suicide?
JA	How many people know?
DC Richardson	I'm just looking at your tribute. You mentioned

that Paul died peacefully in your arms. You never said how he died. You've left that with the reader to surmise.

JA   Yes, it's not a pleasant thing to mention but most people ...

DC Richardson   Most people do know.

JA   Yes.

DC Richardson   You've got friends around the world that you correspond with via the Internet or letters. Are those friends aware that Paul committed suicide as opposed to died?

JA   Yes.

DC Richardson   Right. Have you ever purported that Paul just died of his illness at all, to anyone?

JA   No.

DC Richardson   Right. OK, John.

DC Bosomworth   There are no further questions for the time being. We're going to stop the tape here, consult and probably have a final interview.

JA   Yes.

DC Bosomworth   And that's our intention from now. We'll have a more lengthy break when we finish. Is there anything that you want to add or clarify to what we've spoken about?

JA   No.

DC Bosomworth   Are you happy with that, then?

(Interview concluded in accordance with Codes of Practice)

You will not acquit her because she has never been in trouble with the police; because she has suffered enough; because she has had twenty-two months of this ordeal hanging over her; because he was clearly going to take his life at some stage; because she has been unable to

*grieve or because the last thing, you may conclude, Paul Anderson
would want would be for her to stand in the dock.*

*It is for you to set the standards of the public whom you represent
to decide whether her omission was so bad that she is guilty of
manslaughter. We submit she was a lady who was courageous,
devoted, perhaps some odd ideas, but long suffering and, whatever
else, not a criminal.*

*You determine this case upon the evidence you have heard and
nothing else. We ask you to return a verdict which ends the nightmare
under which she has laboured far too long.*

From the Defence's closing speech

Tape 10: 26 January 2004: 12.28–12.49

DC Bosomworth	Right, as part of the documentation recovered from your house I believe we have got your CV here. Can you just confirm that this is your CV and that you prepared it?
JA	Yes, it is.
DC Bosomworth	When did you prepare that, Jill? Just out of interest.
JA	I actually looked for a job in the area at some point because it was a struggle and we needed more income.
DC Bosomworth	We mentioned to you yesterday that we've been given information from his family that you were married before; possibly in America, and part of your CV actually places you in America, doesn't it?
JA	Yes.

DC Bosomworth   In 1980 to 1982 you were in the San Francisco Bay area.

JA   Yes.

DC Bosomworth   Where did you live there?

JA   It was called Sacramento Street.

DC Bosomworth   And did you live alone?

JA   I shared that apartment with a man. He's in Australia now.

DC Bosomworth   Did you marry that man?

JA   No, Paul was my first and only marriage. I waited thirty-seven years for Paul. He was the only one. So there's nothing to find in America at all. I never, never married there. I would have loved to but I didn't, ever.

DC Bosomworth   I appreciate what you're saying that there's nothing to find there.

JA   No.

DC Bosomworth   I think we've got to look. It's the bottom line really.

JA   If you feel that way.

DC Bosomworth   In 1982 to '84 you worked at a florist.

JA   Yes.

DC Bosomworth   In Brooklyn, New York.

JA   Yes.

DC Bosomworth   Where did you live then?

JA   Well, several addresses, but I was on a street called Seventh Avenue for a while and then I lived on Union Street. This was in Brooklyn.

DC Bosomworth   Again, did you live alone?

JA   No, I was with friends.

DC Bosomworth   Their names?

JA   I can give you my friends that I lived with at

	that time. I can give you names and addresses so you can call them and ask them if I was single.
DC Bosomworth	That wouldn't be a bad idea. Could you do that?
JA	Yes, well you've got my address book.
DC Bosomworth	Right, could you give us the names of the friends?
JA	Yes, Migdalia. She's just moved actually. She's in New Jersey now. I don't even know where I've got her phone number. I will email you or something.
DC Bosomworth	Well, perhaps if you'd like to give it to your solicitor then we'll go through your solicitor.
JA	I can give you all my friends I've lived with in those time periods. There will be no gaps. I've got a friend, Carla, in San Francisco and that's the way to do it, isn't it? Just give you my friends that I lived with.
DC Bosomworth	Yes.
Solicitor	If you give it to me then.
DC Bosomworth	We'll go through your solicitor because I shouldn't have contact with you once you leave this police station and while you're on police bail.
JA	Right.
DC Bosomworth	Because it would be improper, really.
Solicitor	If you send them to me, Jill. I'll pass them on to DC Bosomworth.
JA	My friends will all tell you the same thing, that I never got married in America.
DC Bosomworth	And you were a customer services manager?

JA	Mm.
DC Bosomworth	For the Royal Women's Catalogue?
JA	Yes.
DC Bosomworth	That was between '84 and '86. Were you living in the same area then?
JA	Yes, Brooklyn. Shall I just give you my friends?
DC Bosomworth	Are you able to give the friends' names now or are we going to do that through your solicitor?
Solicitor	As many as possible as she can recall and I'll give them to you.
DC Bosomworth	OK, I'll just finish this bit off here though. Between '86 and '88 you were a marketing representative for a software company in New York?
JA	Yes.
DC Bosomworth	I noticed a gap between 1988 and 1990.
JA	I came back to England because my father was not well and I did temp jobs. Then I got a job at London Weekend Television in September 1989, also on a temporary contract.
DC Bosomworth	Then, in the summer of 1990, you were in Leeds. Was that for two years?
JA	I worked from 1989 to 1992 in television.
DC Bosomworth	Right.
JA	They're all temporary contracts.
DC Bosomworth	Right.
JA	So in order to illustrate that I'd also worked for Yorkshire Television, just for the summer of 1999, then I went back to London, that's how I did my CV.

DC Bosomworth	Oh, right. Is there anything you want to ask about the CV, Mike?
DC Richardson	I was just going to say, Jill, when did you physically return to the UK?
JA	1988.
DC Richardson	Do you know what month or roughly what season?
JA	Around July, August.
DC Richardson	And that was for good?
JA	Yes.
DC Bosomworth	The morning the police came to your house, which was the 18th of July last year.
JA	Yes.
DC Bosomworth	Regarding the death of your husband Paul.
JA	Yes.
DC Bosomworth	The first officer to attend was PO Boulton.
JA	Yes.
DC Bosomworth	PO Boulton. She completed what we call a Report to the Coroner, which is form 68. She basically writes down what's been told to her and the circumstances surrounding her attendance if you like. She said that, initially, you said you discovered the body dead at 10 a.m. but later changed that to 5 a.m. I know we've asked you before but I want to clarify in my own mind why there's a change of time?
JA	I can't . . . I've no idea because, as far as I'm aware, I said Paul turned blue between 5 a.m. and 6 a.m. and he died at 9.30 a.m. so I don't know how that discrepancy's occurred.
DC Bosomworth	She also said that you returned home the previous evening about 6 p.m. and again we . . .

we're not arguing about half an hour here and there, but it says that you told her there was a note on top of him stating, 'I'm sorry, I love you, I can't stand the pain anymore, your darling bear, Paul,' and he was able to hold a mumbled conversation. Is that how you discovered Paul?

JA   Yes.

DC Bosomworth   Was the note on top of Paul?

JA   I don't really remember where it was. I ... when you all entered the house that day I was in the deepest grief. I can't really remember everything that happened. It was ... I went numb when I found him.

DC Bosomworth   But you're not disputing, I take it, that that's what you said to PO Boulton on that day?

JA   I don't know what I said. I was in absolute deep shock. It is the biggest regret of my life, obviously.

DC Bosomworth   What she's saying is that you found the note on top of Paul when you returned home at about 6 p.m.

JA   I found the note and I don't know really where it was. It was possibly on the bed somewhere, or at his side. I'm not really sure.

DC Bosomworth   But you'd seen the note on your return home?

JA   Yes, I had.

DC Bosomworth   Not at some later stage; when you got back and he told you he'd taken enough this time. You saw the note.

JA   Yes.

DC Richardson	And was this at 6:00 or thereabouts?
JA	Oh, I don't know what time I got home. I went out. I'd asked him not to do anything.
DC Richardson	I'm just trying to ascertain that you saw the note on the bed or thereabouts on the bed.
JA	Somewhere.
DC Richardson	At that time, when you returned home from Safeway's at 6:00?
JA	I don't know actually.
Solicitor	No, she doesn't know the precise time, she said.
JA	I don't know the precise time.
DC Richardson	All right then, not the precise time.
JA	I don't know whether I saw it later in the evening or not. It was just a sequence of events.
DC Bosomworth	We're not disputing the time because, as I said, we've not been bothered about half an hour here and there. What I am saying is that PO Boulton is saying that you saw that note on your return home from Safeway's. Is that true or not?
JA	I don't know.
DC Bosomworth	We interviewed you, I think that was on the 31st of July, where you described that Paul had turned blue between 5 and 6 a.m. and you thought, 'Oh my God, he's done it this time and he's gone for the big one.' Yet you still didn't call an ambulance. Why was that?
JA	Because I knew it was too late. If you go blue the poison is running all through your system.

DC Bosomworth	But he was still breathing.
JA	Yes.
DC Bosomworth	You've also mentioned that he stirred a few times or moved his head from side to side throughout the night. Other than asking for his earpiece, did he actually say anything to you?
JA	No.
DC Bosomworth	And if he'd wanted to, do you think he would have awoken?
Solicitor	She can't answer that question.
JA	I can't. I've no idea.
Solicitor	She can't answer that question.
DC Bosomworth	Well, to be fair, she does know how he normally sleeps, whether it be a sleep or a light sleep.
Solicitor	Right, I'm telling her she can't answer that question. It's not a fair and proper question.
DC Bosomworth	In regards to what?
Solicitor	It's not a fair and proper question. It's speculation.
DC Richardson	What were his normal habits, then?
JA	Sometimes, it'd be a deep sleep, sometimes not. He'd been on sleeping medication.

May 1993

We could see deer on the horizon, but we couldn't make out the breed. They moved away, dots of brown and black. 'Fallow deer,' he said, 'or maybe red.'

'That's nice,' my mother said from the back seat of the car. We were taking her to the Isabella Plantation in Richmond Park in London to see the azaleas. We knew they were beautiful in May. We parked and made our way to the garden, to be met by a spectacle of red, pink, white and orange blooms. My mother was a widow and still upset.

'Maybe we could go shopping,' she said.

Paul and I looked at each other. We held hands. She looked in another direction.

'Perhaps we could go to Peter Jones, the John Lewis shop?'

I didn't know what to say as Paul was not keen on shopping. I felt caught between them. 'Look at this flower, amazing,' I said, cupping a large pink azalea in my hand.

My mother stopped and leaned on her heels. 'Yes, they're like the ones at home that Dad planted in the garden,' she said.

I felt a sudden pang that we had inadvertently brought her to a place that reminded her of my father and perhaps that was the source of her irritation and lack of interest. Paul rattled the car keys. We were halfway through the great bank of azaleas that we had waited all week to visit. We returned to the car and drove off, over the bridge into Fulham, through Parson's Green and onto my favourite road.

'Here we are,' I said.

My mother looked out. 'Yes, I remember when you took your brother to see *The Rocky Horror Show* on King's Road when it first came out. Tim Curry,' she said.

'I'd forgotten that, eek a zillion years ago. He's never been the same since.'

'Tim?'

'No, my brother.'

Paul smiled as he drove.

'As everyone knows, he never really recovered from when my sister and I put make-up on him when he was two.'

'I shouldn't have gone out,' my mother said dryly.

The glamour boutiques and art shops of King's Road flashed past. The street looked as well kept and as special as ever. We found a place to park near the department store at the very end of King's Road on the corner of Sloane Square.

'It's gone up,' I said as I pumped coins into the meter.

Paul scraped his heels on the pavement and straightened his collar. He talked to my mother.

'Your hair looks nice.'

My mother looked in her bag, then at him and went into the department store. We followed in her wake. She had entered eight floors of retail heaven. The glassy, 1930s building felt as if it had stood there for centuries. I saw my mother's shoulders relax as she made her way purposefully to the furnishings department. She was on home ground. Paul and I lagged behind.

Her hands ran over curtain fabric; she touched cushions and tested them for softness. She bought some cotton serviettes. Paul had left us and was wandering through the clock section. He had become entranced by a cuckoo clock. I followed my mother. A woman brushed against me.

'Jill.'

I turned.

'Hello, long time no see,' she said.

'Samantha, good to see you. This is my mother, my boyfriend is ... somewhere.' My mother greeted Samantha as I scanned the shop for him. He had his back to us in a far corner in the lighting section. My mother fiddled with her handbag as I talked. Samantha was in a hurry.

Paul arrived. He had something in a store bag. I reached for it but he held it away from me. I stood on tiptoe and the bag went higher. We kissed. My mother headed for a book of wallpaper samples.

'Give.'

'No.' He whisked the bag out of my reach. 'Later.'

That night, when my mother was settled in our bed and we were on the blow-up bed in the hallway, I opened his gift. A pair of black leather gloves, something I had always wanted. They were as soft as kidskin. The softest black leather I had ever felt.

Tape 10: 26 January 2004: 12.28–12.49 continued

DC Bosomworth	When I attended your house on the afternoon of the 18th.
JA	Yes.
DC Bosomworth	I took a statement from you regarding the circumstances surrounding Paul's death.
JA	Yes.
DC Bosomworth	I have this statement here. First of all, Jill, can I confirm that this is your signature?
JA	Yes.
DC Bosomworth	And it's your signature on all the pages?
JA	Yes.
DC Bosomworth	At the top of the first page there's a declaration, yes?
JA	Yes.
DC Bosomworth	Would you read that out for me, please?
JA	This statement, consisting of four pages each signed by me, is true and to the best of my knowledge and belief. I make it knowing that, if it is tendered in evidence, I shall be liable to prosecution if I have wilfully stated anything in it, which I know to be false, or do not believe to be true.

DC Bosomworth   Thank you. Do you recall making this statement?

JA   I recall making the statement and, due to the circumstances, you came to the cottage and you introduced yourself as Mr Nasty and I was in the deepest grief and shock. You took me outside to the garden and proceeded to interview me. We made that statement together. You asked me at the end of that particular interview to sign the statement, comprising four and a half written pages. You asked me if I would like to read it and foolishly I did not. I just signed it.

DC Bosomworth   Right, could I . . .

JA   So I actually don't know what is written on those pages.

DC Bosomworth   Can I just clarify two points then first of all. The first point is that I don't think I introduced myself as Mr Nasty. I think I said I would have some nasty questions to ask you and they would be the worst part really of us being there at that time. Do you agree with that or not?

JA   I don't know, I just heard Mr Nasty.

DC Bosomworth   All right and that you were indeed given the opportunity. I gave you the opportunity to read this statement. I mean you've nodded there.

JA   Yes.

DC Bosomworth   Again, Jill.

JA   Yes, you did give me the opportunity and I didn't, so I don't know what is in the

statement. I was in deep, deep shock and
grief when this happened to me.

DC Bosomworth ·I'm going to read you a section of this statement then I'm going to give you the
opportunity yourself to read that section. I
don't wish to go through the whole statement
because some of it is actually about the background of Paul's illness.

JA   Yes.

DC Bosomworth Which I think we've discussed at length.

August 1998

A hot summer's day and the trees were ragged and dry. The
deep greens had crackling edges of grey and the branches
were starting to release their leaves. The grass was full of
crickets and crinkled under our feet as we walked by the riverbank. The water in the river was low and red-brown from
iron deposits. I listened as he described the boat he planned
to build me. Instead, we had a blow-up rubber raft with two
yellow plastic oars. This was to become our Riviera, on the
riverbanks of the Ure near Leyburn, not far from where we
lived.

The straps of the rucksack dug into my shoulders and the
large bag with the raft in it seemed to get heavier and heavier.
And yet he walked, it seemed, casually in front of me carrying
the oars. 'Can't you help me carry any of this?' I wanted to say
to him. I clamped my mouth shut. I stopped, dropped the bag
and stretched my hands. He carried on walking ahead, searching
for a spot to pitch and picnic. The bank had a dense line of trees
along it. Where there were gaps, other people were already
occupying them. The great English Sunday jaunt. I passed a

vacant slot, and called him back. He looked at me and the cleft in the bank.

'It's too small and there's nowhere to launch. It's too steep,' he said.

I looked at the incline and realized that he was right. 'I'm fed up of carrying all this,' I said.

He gazed at me. The sky was blank white. He was covered in sweat even though it was not that hot. I was carrying everything and hardly sweating at all.

'I would if I could,' he said. 'Come on, packhorse, we'll find somewhere. It'll be worth it.'

I resigned myself to another one of his expeditions. Why did he have to go one extra mile? We carried on walking. He stopped to examine a bush with pink bell-shaped flowers. He picked one and showed me the helmet, saying, '*Impatiens glandulifera.*' I crossed my eyes. We passed through a row of trees that grew right down to the bank. Beyond them, the riverbank seemed to open up, with fewer trees clustered to the edge. Yet the bank was still 5 to 10 feet high. Where were the gentle slopes? My feet ached. I was really starting to get irritated. Then we found the spot simultaneously. The bank had gradually started to roll down to the water and mossy grass dusted the slope.

He watched me as I pumped up the raft. I stopped myself saying anything. I had to remind myself that energy conservation was part of his body-management scheme. We were not on the water long. It probably took longer to inflate the raft.

I let my hand drift in the water as he rowed. He tried to keep us out of the thick scrolls of bulrush that lined the river on both banks. Then his arms sank to his sides and he held the oars limply. His face was covered in perspiration. It was my turn. We got back somehow. He clambered out of the raft and got back to the picnic rug. 'You're rubbish at rowing,' he said.

He lay down on the picnic rug. It was a standard woollen Scottish tartan. I dragged the raft out of the water and pulled the plug. It was flat in a few moments. He watched. Great swathes of gnats hovered above his head. The reeds rattled against the river-bank. He poured me a cup of tea from our flask and I unwrapped the tomato and ham sandwiches. He talked about the fish lying in the deep water having a kip or cruising for a bite. There would be pike here. I told him about the newspaper article I had read. A boy had almost lost his hand recently to a 30-pound pike. The one they were all trying to catch; the one the anglers called 'Big Red'. The general agreement was that it had to be him, judging by the bite mark left on the boy's hand. The Sunday afternoon drifted by.

By late afternoon, it was time to return to the car. We gathered our gear. We were both tired. We walked past a group of people, about ten women and men, mainly men. They were fishing. He wanted to stop. I did not.

'I want to get home,' I said, 'I've got to cook dinner.' He ignored me.

The men were hauling out ugly eels, some of them 3 to 6 feet long, and chunky. I wondered if they were really going to eat them. I had had jellied eels once in the East End of London. They were sour, like bad sardines. He started talking to the group, who turned out to be Polish visitors. When he found out, he switched to their mother tongue. I tried to smile at them. They had taken to him and gathered round. I stood on the edge of the group and checked my watch. I had no idea what he was talking about. As we left, they were acting like he was an old friend. In the car on the way home, he told me that one of them had asked what part of Poland he came from.

I squinted into the receding sun. It was dipping closer to the horizon of hills. It was milky and hazy. The birds had stopped singing. It would be dark soon.

Tape 10: 26 January 2004: 12.28–12.49 continued

DC Bosomworth   The first bit I'll read out is about the time of 5 a.m.: 'Paul had turned blue and I knew he hadn't made it. Paul told me yesterday that his love for me had kept him going and he wished I didn't love him so much. I knew he was going to take his own life and I knew he didn't want me to stop him or call for any assistance as he'd been through this twice before only to recover and carry on in pain.' The section I've read out, Jill, starts there. If you'd like to confirm that is what it actually says.

JA   I don't obviously recall ever . . .

Solicitor   Just confirm whether that's what it actually says to start with.

JA   Well, yes, that's what it says, but I don't ever recall saying that to you. You have written it down obviously. I don't recall those events and I knew Paul told me that he loved me and wished I didn't love him so much. But I don't really believe that I knew he was going to take his own life and that he didn't want me to stop him.

DC Bosomworth   Right.

JA   He caught me off guard that day and I went numb. I had asked him not to do anything and when I came back he had. But I didn't know how much he had taken and I just hoped he was going to sleep it off.

DC Bosomworth	Well, the first thing is that you've confirmed that that's what's in the statement.
JA	Yes.
DC Bosomworth	And I've got to say it isn't something I've made up and I hope there's no suggestion that you haven't said that to me when I've written it down.
JA	I don't know. I was in very deep shock and I don't think I was in a fit state to be interviewed, that's my assessment of this situation.
DC Bosomworth	Well, I took the statement and it was a statement on what you told me that day. And I think it's a pertinent passage in this four-page statement. Had Paul told you the day before that your love for him kept him going?
JA	He was constantly telling me that. It wasn't just the day before, it was constant, constantly throughout our relationship. That's the basis of the relationship. It's a love story.
DC Bosomworth	Did you know he was going to take his own life?
JA	No, I didn't.
DC Bosomworth	And did you know that he didn't want you to stop him if he did?
JA	No, I wasn't sure how much he'd taken and I went into massive shock and I realize that now.
DC Bosomworth	So, for whatever reasons, whether it was because you were in shock or whatever, this passage in this statement is not true?
JA	I would dispute it now because I was in

shock. I don't think I was thinking straight at all when you came that day.

DC Bosomworth Yes, you've stated you were in shock. We aren't looking to investigate you for offences of perverting the course of justice or attempting to. I'm asking you if now, today, you believe that passage to be true.

JA   Can I interrupt the interview and talk to my solicitor, please?

DC Bosomworth Yes. What I'll do is give the time out and then we'll continue the interview with another set of tapes, is that OK? The time by my watch is 12.49 p.m.

At three that afternoon, the detective constable comes. He would not have taken a statement from her if he felt she was just so overcome, so beside herself, that she could not concentrate and give rational, careful consideration to what she wanted to say. So he was satisfied. She signs the caption. She signs every page. She signs the mistake that had been made somewhere. She signs the end of it. Whether it is read to her, or whether she reads it. That is what she said. You may have no doubt about that. You have the clearest evidence of the officer on that.

From the Defence's closing speech

Tape 11: 26 January 2004: 13.02–13.30

DC Bosomworth We called a break in the last interview because you wanted to consult with your solicitor, is that correct?

JA   Yes.

DC Bosomworth   OK, is it right that you and Paul married on the 25th of February, oh sorry, that Paul was born on the 25th February 1960?

JA   Yes.

DC Bosomworth   And that three days before you got married, he contracted a virus?

JA   It was about that time, yes.

DC Bosomworth   And when did you actually get married then, Jill?

JA   I believe it was on the 24th of March 1995.

DC Bosomworth   OK, and did Paul have a series of tests around 1997 and '98?

JA   Yes.

DC Bosomworth   Right.

JA   Which was actually documented with his Chronic Fatigue Syndrome.

DC Bosomworth   And was it around that time that he was diagnosed as having post-viral disability?

JA   '97, '98.

DC Bosomworth   I'm going to ask you, Jill. I mean, these are facts that I wouldn't readily know.

JA   That's correct and I agree with you.

DC Bosomworth   You know, yeah.

JA   And I understand now that I said those things. I made a statement to you because I was in deep emotional shock. It wasn't the right time and my mind was in complete turmoil and I didn't read the statement but I'm not disputing that that's what I said.

DC Bosomworth   But you're not disputing that you were given the opportunity to read that statement.

JA   I was given the opportunity but I was in deep shock and my mind was in absolute turmoil. I don't think I was thinking straight at all when I gave you that statement.

DC Bosomworth OK, the passage that was in dispute which you've read and I've read out.

JA Yes.

DC Bosomworth I'm going to go through that again, Jill.

JA Yes.

DC Bosomworth The reason I did the first part, if you like, the initial page, was that I wanted to show you that you'd told me facts I couldn't possibly have known.

JA Yes.

DC Bosomworth Myself.

JA Agreed.

DC Bosomworth And that I wasn't really in a position to add things to your statement.

JA Yes, I understand.

DC Bosomworth And I've got to say, I don't like the idea that people may think I've added stuff in your statement that you haven't told me.

JA I'm sorry. I didn't mean to imply that, it's just my state of mind.

DC Bosomworth It's OK. The passage I actually read out, and that you read, said that at around 5 a.m. Paul had turned blue and you knew he hadn't made it. You went on to say that 'Paul told me yesterday that his love for me kept him going and he wished I didn't love him so much. I knew he was going to take his own life and I know he didn't want me to stop him or call for any assistance as he'd been through this twice before only to recover and carry on in pain.' I'm going to show you it again where I've started reading, there, at 5 a.m. We're not disputing that passage is in the statement.

JA   I'm not disputing it.

March 1993

The music started low and then got louder and louder. We were at Sonia's flat in Hammersmith. She had only invited a few people, but word had got out and her flat was filled wall to wall. She did not know most of them. We were gyrating somewhere in the middle. Our bodies smacked together and elbows and legs got tangled with ours as we danced.

'I need some air,' I said.

He smiled and guided me. We got distracted by different conversations on the way out.

'Yeah, I was at a party once where there were so many people that some of us ended up on the roof looking at the stars.'

'That was a party.'

'The cops came.'

'What for?'

'They told us to turn it down – or they'd do us for breach of the peace.'

'So did you?'

'We had to.'

'Where was that, then?'

We got out of the flat and squeezed past bodies on the stairs. Sonia's neighbours had joined in and the foundations of the building were thumping. We stepped out onto the street, which stretched down to the river. Charing Cross Hospital lay in the other direction. We stood around talking with a few other party-goers as we cooled off. Sweat trickled down us. Some of them were drinking out of cans, bottles or paper cups.

'I met a bird and she came on to me. I mean she must have been over forty. I ran for my life.'

'I was putting a nail in and water came out. Hit the wrong pipe. Christmas Eve.'

'Called Jack the other night, he was . . .'

'I just think politics does not exist in this country anymore. I mean, what happened to feminism?'

Paul got into a discussion about snooker. I was bored. I left him chatting to a lad with wavy hair and a bruised eye. I squeezed past a gaggle of girls in tight tops with dark eye shadow and lashings of mascara. One of them was drunk and the others were helping her down the stairs. I walked back into the party and headed for the bathroom. There was a queue. The woman next to me turned: 'I think someone is being sick in there,' she said.

I decided to aim for the kitchen. It was tiny. The floor was wet and sticky. Two people were snogging in a corner. A large man in his early thirties was sipping Carling Black Label from a can and groping a young woman next to him. The kitchen table was covered in empty wine bottles. I picked one or two up just to make sure. He was driving. There was a bottle of cider. I poured a small glass. Someone tapped me on the shoulder.

'Are you mixing?'

It was him.

'Nah.' I put the glass down.

Sonia came in. She was drunk and her face was flushed. She put her arms around us. 'I love both of you.' She kissed us on the cheeks, and squeezed us. 'Come, come and dance.' She pulled us into the lounge and started shaking her body to the music. It blasted away and we all moved to the beat.

'*Gotta be startin' somethin', I said you wanna be startin' somethin'* ...'

We left about 4 a.m. and cruised home. The streets were glassy. It had rained hard. We splashed through puddles. We pulled over at a kebab house and ate something, chewing slowly, then continued.

We put the key into the lock of our front door at around 5.30 a.m. The birds were starting to sing in the half dawn.

Tape 11: 26 January 2004: 13.02–13.30 continued

DC Bosomworth	OK then, Jill.
JA	So I don't think my mind was working properly at all.
DC Bosomworth	Right, but you aren't disputing what has been said.
JA	No.
DC Bosomworth	Right, in that case, you've given me, or you've given PC Boulton and myself, if you like, differing accounts of what happened.
JA	Yes, because.
DC Bosomworth	No, no.
JA	Yes and you know the reasons why.
DC Bosomworth	Yes, I accept that, so what I'm going to ask you to do now then, and I know it's several months later ...
JA	Yes.
DC Bosomworth	Is to actually give me your account now as to what happened on the evening of the 17th when you said you went to Pateley Bridge to get a pizza and returned because you were worried.

JA   Yes.

DC Bosomworth   Right, I think you said to me, and I will be corrected, that you'd been making or writing the list of Paul's illnesses in order to make a claim and that actually got him down on the 17th.

JA   Well, I think, if you read the list it would get anyone down, but I can't remember him being down. He wasn't a down person actually, he was incredibly positive, which astonished me about him.

DC Bosomworth   So take me through it then, Jill.

JA   Yes.

DC Bosomworth   Right. You said, Jill, that when you got back and he was sitting on the side of the bed.

JA   Yes.

DC Bosomworth   Which side of the bed would that be?

JA   It was his side, nearest the window, I think. I think it was the left-hand side.

DC Bosomworth   And was he clothed?

JA   He had his pyjamas on.

DC Bosomworth   And he collapsed and went to sleep.

JA   Yes.

DC Bosomworth   Did you cover him up at this point? Because, when we arrived he was lying in the foetal position. Was that how he normally slept?

JA   I went numb. I couldn't actually recall.

DC Bosomworth   You know what I mean by the foetal position, lying on your side?

JA   Yes, I do. He slept in all different positions.

DC Bosomworth   Did he, at times, have difficulty making it to

	the toilet?
JA	Oh yes, and I would take him. I did every-thing for him, whatever he wanted.
DC Bosomworth	I meant making it to the toilet in time, actu-ally.
JA	Oh no, no, not at all, but he had terrible kidney pains and I wrapped a duvet around him to keep his kidneys warm, because he had terrible kidney spasms.
DC Bosomworth	Was that during the night?
JA	Yes.
DC Bosomworth	So, at some point then, you actually covered him, didn't you?
JA	Yes, I must have done. Yes, wrapped him up.
DC Bosomworth	I never have and I'm still not disputing your love for Paul. Do you know at what point you actually covered him?
JA	I've no idea.
DC Bosomworth	Because, I'm just thinking, if someone sat on the side of the bed and collapsed then they're not going to be covered.
JA	I know, so I must have wrapped him because I kept him nice and toasty.
DC Bosomworth	And I believe you had a towel around his bottom half.
JA	Yes, because he had these terrible kidney pains and it would keep him warm and everything.
DC Bosomworth	Did you place that around him, then?
JA	I must have done. I don't know how things happened.
DC Bosomworth	Sorry.

JA	I don't know. I can't remember, you know, I was in shock.
DC Bosomworth	Right, I mean, I don't think there's any dispute that he had a towel wrapped around his bottom half. I forget the colour, but I believe it was possibly blue.
JA	I don't have any blue towels.
DC Bosomworth	No. He did have a towel around his bottom half.
JA	I don't know.
DC Bosomworth	You said that you never assisted him in suicide.
JA	No.
DC Bosomworth	And it was his decision. His own decision.
JA	Yes.
DC Bosomworth	That's what I mean.
JA	That was by his own hand, yes.
DC Bosomworth	You talked fairly quickly for me but I have actually written down the words, 'it was his own decision'. It was his decision to take his life.
JA	Yes, and there was no discussion. He caught me off guard. Obviously, I couldn't do twenty-four-hour suicide watch. He had made two other attempts. I had called an ambulance. He'd had a situation in the garage which I described to you earlier and you must have that hosepipe with both our fingerprints on it and I just saved his life.
DC Bosomworth	Right, Jill, we haven't got the hosepipe with the fingerprints on it, but I haven't disputed what happened in the garage, all right.
JA	Mmmm. I begged him and I got him back

	into the cottage.
DC Bosomworth	OK.
JA	So this is a difficult situation, isn't it?
DC Bosomworth	And again I've written down that you were hoping he hadn't taken any. I'm assuming you mean tablets by that, do you?
JA	Yes, I was hoping. I was hoping he hadn't taken enough. I knew he had taken some because I told you that.
DC Bosomworth	And we're talking morphine basically, are we?
JA	We must be, yes.
DC Bosomworth	Sorry, Jill, you say 'must be' but he had several lots of medication.
JA	He had a lot of medication all over the place.
DC Bosomworth	So why do you say it must have been morphine, then?
JA	I would have thought it was. He was on morphine, Zopiclone, all kinds of medication over the years that he'd been collecting.
DC Bosomworth	You said you hoped he hadn't taken enough, so you knew he had taken some.
JA	Yes.
DC Bosomworth	So, I suppose, my next question is, you came back, you were hoping he hadn't taken enough, yet he collapsed as he was sitting on the side of the bed.
JA	Yes.
DC Bosomworth	And gone into a sleep.
JA	Yes.
DC Bosomworth	Why didn't you contact the ambulance service at that point?

JA	Well, I wasn't sure. I just thought I'd let him sleep it off. He had a bit of whisky and he'd done this before. You never think it's going to happen. You just never think.
DC Bosomworth	But the words you used is that he collapsed.
JA	I don't know, in a way he just fell into a nice sleep, just waited for me and that was it.
DC Bosomworth	I mean alarm bells were ringing, were they not, when you went to Pateley Bridge?
JA	No, no, no. I was just concerned about him. I wouldn't say alarm bells. I just had to make sure he was all right, but, as I said, I couldn't do twenty-four-hour suicide watch. He was at risk. But I never, never thought he was going to do it. I saved him twice before and he hadn't taken enough in those other attempts. I just kept thinking he wouldn't have taken enough.
DC Bosomworth	So why did you turn back from Pateley Bridge?
JA	Because I was worried about him and concerned. I just wanted to check on him.
DC Bosomworth	And what was the worry?
JA	Just to make sure he was all right.
DC Bosomworth	As regards?
JA	Just to make sure that he was all right and alive and whatever, I don't know what can I tell you?
DC Bosomworth	I mean, you used the word 'alive' there.
JA	Yes.
DC Bosomworth	I mean, had it crossed your mind that he was

going to attempt suicide while you went to Pateley Bridge?

JA No. I just don't know what I was thinking. I just wanted to make sure he was all right and I've done this before. I'd start journeys and come back to see. I was dedicated to saving his life.

DC Bosomworth Somewhere I have read, and I can't put my hand straight on it, that, at some point, you have certainly told either PO Boulton and myself that you turned back from Pateley Bridge. You went and spoke to him and he assured you basically that he hadn't done anything. Is that now not the case?

JA He told me. I got back and he promised me that he wasn't going to do anything, that everything was fine and not to worry about him, but I was worried all the time. During the last six months he was just declining further and neither of us could stop it. We had got the morphine for him and we couldn't think of anything else but the pain was increasing, not decreasing, so the amount of stress and pressure I was under was unbelievable. I realize that now ... I trusted him.

DC Bosomworth You were hoping but you didn't actually know.

JA No, I didn't and it caught me off guard. I'd called twice before and it had proved to be a wasted journey on both occasions because, if you check his hospital records, he hadn't taken enough. He wouldn't have died. They didn't need to do anything. They just put him on the machines and did tests. I was hoping it would be like that this time and it wasn't.

DC Bosomworth You said ...

JA And he left suicide notes before.

DC Bosomworth You described how you were his carer.

JA Yes.

DC Bosomworth And indeed ...

JA And I stated that to him.

DC Bosomworth And on at least two occasions in order to keep him alive you sought help. Don't you think, Jill, you had a responsibility when you discovered on your return home he'd taken tablets that perhaps you should have contacted the emergency services? And that when you found the suicide note perhaps you should have contacted the emergency services? And when he had turned blue?

JA In hindsight, I should have called the ambulance. I went into shock. I didn't think he'd taken an overdose.

DC Bosomworth You used a term yourself, 'assisted suicide'. What do you know about assisted suicide?

JA I know nothing at all and I never assisted him.

DC Bosomworth It wasn't the case that when you got back from Pateley Bridge, well from going to Pateley Bridge because you never actually got there, and you spoke to Paul, that you actually left him, knowing that he was going

	to take those tablets and you went out of the house to be out of the way?
JA	No, never. He caught me off guard that day.
DC Richardson	Jill, you mentioned that you weren't sure whether he had taken enough.
JA	That's right.
DC Richardson	You also said that you went to the cabinet to see how much he'd taken but you couldn't do it.
JA	I couldn't get there, no.
DC Richardson	Is it not fair to say that you had the opportunity to ascertain whether he had taken enough from the cabinet?
JA	Yes, but I actually wouldn't have known because the cabinet was always heaped up with pills so I wouldn't have known what he'd taken and what he hadn't.
DC Richardson	Bearing in mind that you collect his medication, such as morphine.
JA	Yes.
DC Richardson	And are you aware that he self-medicated?
JA	Yes.
DC Richardson	You had already said that you were going to the cabinet to see how much he had taken, so you had it in your mind that you could possibly find out how much, but you couldn't do it.
JA	I suppose so. Yes, I didn't.
DC Richardson	Why couldn't you do it?
JA	I don't know. I just went numb this time. I'm sorry, that's the wrong word to use.

DC Richardson	Jill, I'm going to put a scenario to you that Paul, obviously, as we know, was in pain. He was in absolute agony and it hurt. You were hurting watching your loved one suffer so much. You were aware that this was happening. Paul couldn't take it anymore and he wanted to go. He wanted to go and get rid of the pain. Wilfully, knowingly, or otherwise, you saw that he had taken steps to end his own life and that you didn't do anything to prevent him dying. Is that the case?
JA	I don't think so. I didn't want to believe that. It's been a terribly long battle. I was exhausted with worry and, looking at the sequence of events, I just trusted that he wouldn't have taken enough and that he would wake up and he didn't. I've got to live with it for the rest of my life, haven't I, and that's punishment enough.
DC Richardson	I'm not here to judge you, that's not my job.
JA	I know. I appreciate that.
DC Richardson	And I can see the horrible situation that you were in and Paul as well. That's my personal view and I've got to take that aside.
JA	Yes.
DC Richardson	I've got to try and ascertain what happened. You told us about the events. What we aren't getting to very well is what you were thinking.
JA	I don't know what I was thinking. I've no

idea. I was thinking, I've got to get the food in and then I've got to cook it for him. I told him that I would give him a massage because I massaged him every day and I said, 'Just wait for me and I'll give you a massage.'

DC Richardson   Do you recall at any point making a conscious decision?

JA   So I was thinking about cooking and this, that and the other, actually.

July 2000

I crunched through the shorn stubbles, jaggedly mown. The long grass was cut, honeyed, silky, bound into golden bales. It was before twilight, the descending sun on my back; warm stillness. I imagined what it was like a hundred years ago, the hay coming in, the shire horses' feet stamping as young men pitched it into carts. Young girls bringing flagons of ale to them. The chaff, sweat, dust on their burnished foreheads as they drank deeply.

I wandered across the landlord's field where he had been cutting and turning the hay for three days, before the balers with their machines came. The field was dotted with bales and an intoxicating smell of freshly cut grass. A thistle thrush called somewhere with its long throaty gurgle.

I reached him on the banks of a small river at the bottom of the long field. He stood among the trees there with his back to me, motionless, on tiptoes, right at the edge of the bank. The water was low now in the summer. I could see his frame, small shoulders which were slightly hunched. A twig cracked under my foot. I approached him and he turned with a smile on his face.

'Snug,' he said.

'Yes.'

'I've caught one.'

'Great.'

I went to him, put my arms around his waist and leaned on him. I held him so he would not fall. We smiled as we swayed. His line was out in the river. The evening flight insects swam around us, hunting. The line drifted with the current.

'Where is it?' I said.

'I put it back. It was a tiny baby, so I released it.'

'Your first fish.'

'Yes, he was too young to keep.'

We smiled. I sat down next to him and he continued fishing. The sun was lower now.

'Dark soon,' I said.

'Yes.'

'No trout for me to cook tonight, then.'

'No.'

'I'll find something for us. I think I've got some barbecue ribs. Will they do?'

'Lovely.'

A heron glided above us. Its wide wings spread like sails. Its long neck stretched. He was our local heron.

'There he goes,' I said.

'Yes.' He looked up.

'Are you coming home soon?'

'Just a wee bit longer.'

I got up and walked across the fields again, stopping at the edge of the garden. I could smell the nicotiana. Its rich, sweet, treacly scent made me fall in love every summer. I turned to see if he was behind me. Not yet. The sun was on the horizon and almost gone. A bat banked past me. I turned again, home.

Tape 11: 26 January 2004: 13.02–13.30 continued

DC Richardson	But then you're confronted with this scenario where you're aware that Paul had taken tablets. You had the opportunity to find out if he'd taken enough.
JA	I wouldn't know because, as I've said, the cabinet was always heaped with tablets, so I wouldn't know whether it was enough or not.
DC Richardson	But I'm referring to what you said, Jill. You said you went to the cabinet to see how much he'd taken, but couldn't do it, so you were aware when you went there that you could find out how much he'd taken.
JA	No. I don't think so. I would try to go and look but then I wouldn't have been able to work it out anyway, if I think about it.

October 2002

The pumpkin was bright, bright orange. He rolled it around in his hands, looking for places to carve the eyes, nose and mouth. He put it on the bed and started work with his hunting knife. He cut triangles for the eyes and an oblong for the nose. Then he carefully carved a mouth with teeth. When he was satisfied with his creation, he carried it to the chest of drawers, placed it on top and put a candle inside.

In the evening we watched it glow. We settled into bed next to each other. It was cold outside. He switched on the radio and searched for ghost stories. He placed my radio earpiece in my ear for me. He found *The Turn of the Screw* — we listened as the narrator inflected his voice from creepy to ghostly. I snuggled closer to him. The pumpkin spread light up the wall and onto the ceiling. He turned the dial on the radio again and found a show with callers telling the host about their encounters with the supernatural. The words drifted through me.

'We were driving through a forest with some friends on a narrow road. Suddenly a black vintage car appeared, coming really fast at us in the other direction. I tried to swerve, but the road was narrow and there were trees everywhere. The car was on top of us and went straight through us. All we could see were blood-red eyes.'

'It was a country road, and me, the missus and the kids were looking for blackberries and the like. It was bright, you know, sunny, and then it all went black. We couldn't see anything in front or behind. I've never been so scared. All we could hear was a wolf-like sound. We clutched each other.'

'A figure stood at the end of my bed, bloodless. It's cruel eyes looked at me as if into my very being. I shut my eyes, and opened them. A long, splindly hand drained of blood pointed at me. It had a hollow look. Its thin lips moved. It moved towards me. I pulled the sheets around me, but it yanked them off me. A shrill cry came from somewhere inside me, but there was no sound. The curtains in the window suddenly blew as if there was a howling gale. The bloodless figure moved closer. I could smell a ghastly stench. I watched as its shape changed into a black moving shadow that crept up the wall and spread across the ceiling above me.

'"What do you want?" I managed to say.

'An unearthly voice answered, "You."

'I heard a crash somewhere and it was gone. I got up, trembling. My nightie had shrivelled. I went downstairs and saw that all the cupboards in my kitchen were open and all my china and pots had been thrown out and lay smashed in heaps on the floor. The kitchen table was turned upside down. My husband came home from work. He's a night porter. We soon moved out of that house, and I'll never go down that street, ever again.'

I looked over at the pumpkin. The wax was overflowing and pouring down the front of the drawers. I jumped out of bed and grabbed a towel from the radiator to stop the flow before it reached the carpet. But there were already a few spots of wax on it. I would iron them out with brown paper. I returned to bed and waited for the wax to cool and harden. We giggled at the sight of the pumpkin: it had sagged.

We continued with our journey through ghoul land. Later, I broke the wax and threw it away. Paul got up and put a torch inside the pumpkin, and it was alive again. We fell asleep, listening to stories wrapped in each other's arms.

Tape 11: 26 January 2004: 13.02–13.30 continued

DC Richardson	But why couldn't you do it?
JA	I just . . .
Solicitor	Well, she's told you that now, twice.
JA	Yes, I went numb.
DC Richardson	You went numb and that was the reason that you couldn't do it?
JA	Yes.
DC Richardson	Is it possible that you couldn't do it because you didn't want to know whether he'd taken enough to take his own life?
JA	I don't know.

DC Richardson	Did you make a conscious decision not to do it for that reason?
JA	I don't know. You know the answer, don't you? In hindsight, I should have called the ambulance and I didn't.
DC Bosomworth	Is there anything you want to add, Jill?
Solicitor	No, on my advice, no. Nothing else to say. We've said enough and it's been going on for too long. I think, with all due respect, you know we're in a situation where you're trying to wear her down and she's not having it.
DC Bosomworth	I don't think that comment's quite fair. We've ended the interview and I've just asked Jill if there's anything else she wants to add.
Solicitor	Well, on my advice there's nothing else that she wants to say.

It is so simple to pick up the phone and dial '999' that you may say to yourself, 'Why on earth didn't she do it?' We know she loved him. The only answer, we submit, on the evidence, is because she knew he wanted to go . . . to die, in dignity.

From the Defence's closing speech

Epilogue

April 2005

On 20 April 2005, Jill Anderson went on trial for manslaughter at Leeds Crown Court. By this time she had been on police bail for almost two years. She had been arrested for manslaughter and assisted suicide in July 2003, twelve days after Paul died. Three days of police interrogation followed at Harrogate Police Station. In September 2004, Jill was told to report back to the police station, where she was charged with manslaughter. The charge of assisted suicide had been dropped, because the authorities could not find any evidence that Jill had assisted Paul to take his own life. In fact, she had done everything to prevent this. If convicted, Jill could now face up to fifteen years in prison. She surrendered her passport and had to report weekly to the police station. Three times, she went to court in an attempt to reduce the conditions of her bail. She was also ordered not to contact or speak to Paul's family.

The court case was preceded by a four-day predirectional hearing at which the Defence tried to stop the case proceeding. Since this was potentially a test case, these attempts were rejected by Judge Geoffrey Grigson. Instead he ruled that the case should be tried by jury. So, over the next six days, the intimate details of Jill's relationship with her husband were picked over by the Prosecution team, led by David Perry QC, and the Defence team, led by Paul Worsley QC, while a jury of eight men and four women looked on. Jill did not take the stand herself as she was deemed unfit, having been diagnosed by her doctor as suffering from depression and exhaustion. The jury retired to consider the evidence and returned in just two hours to give a verdict of 'not guilty'.

Outside the courtroom, Jill's solicitor gave the following statement:

> For the last twenty-two months, Jill Anderson has had to endure the death of her husband, the ignominy of being arrested, an interminable police inquiry and now a trial. By the verdict of the jury this afternoon her actions of 17th and 18th July 2003 have been totally vindicated. She did what she thought was right and proper and, more importantly, what she believed her husband would have wished. She now needs time to reflect, to regain her health and to grieve, something which hitherto she has been prevented from doing. She wishes for nothing more than to be able to rebuild her life.

Paul's relatives expressed a different view: 'We are naturally disappointed with the outcome. Paul's death was unnecessary. The one person to whom he entrusted his care let him down. By any standards of human behaviour we believe that Jill's actions in failing to summon medical assistance were morally unforgiveable.' They also described as 'cruel' her decision not to inform the family of his death until six months later.

During the eight years of Paul's illness, he was seen by over thirty-five doctors and consultants in eight different hospitals. Since his death, there has been a change in the approach of the medical profession towards myalgic encephalomyelitis (ME)/Chronic Fatigue Syndrome (CFS) and there is now a centre specializing in ME/CFS in West Yorkshire. More research needs to be done, however, particularly in reference to the depression that is suffered by many people with chronic physical diseases.

Shortly after the trial, Jill Anderson moved to Exeter in an attempt to put these tragic events behind her and to start a new life. She also decided to write this memoir about her experiences and to work towards giving a higher profile to the disease.

March 1995

I was standing with one leg in and one leg out of my tights. The polish on my fingernails was not dry. I snagged the nylon. I brushed past him. We were in the living room of our studio flat. It was a mess. I yanked at a drawer in one of our wardrobes, sending knickers and tights flying everywhere, as I searched for a new pair, muttering and cursing under my breath. He came up to me and asked if the knot in his tie was straight. I jiggled it a bit. He went back to the mirror.

'You've messed up,' he said.

'Have not.'

'So have.'

'I can't find any new tights,' I said, 'the taxi will be here in a minute.'

The doorbell rang. We looked at each other and ran around frantically grabbing what we needed. My handbag, his wallet, this and that. The doorbell rang again.

He went to the intercom and buzzed the person in as I tried to make my curly hair stick down. I jammed a hat on it. A straw boater affair with navy edging around the brim and navy ribbon on the crown. I straightened my light blue silk suit once more and twisted and turned in front of the mirror, looking for bumps in my figure.

'More flowers,' he said, returning from the door.

We both collapsed on the sofa and looked at each other. He was wearing a light grey wool suit with faint red and blue threads woven through. We had bought both outfits a few days earlier at a shopping mall in Kingston, talking excitedly all the way there and all the way back.

Our flat was festooned with cards and flowers. We had so many bouquets from family and friends that we had run out of vases. A bouquet of lilies, roses, alstroemeria and iris from his elder sister lay between us on the sofa. The telephone rang again. It had not stopped all morning with calls from well-wishers.

The taxi arrived. We clambered in and arrived on King's Road in Chelsea around noon. The normally busy street seemed slow and lethargic today. It was a decent day for March and not raining. The sun was drifting in and out among the buildings. The sky was a light blue to match my suit. We looked for a pub and found one nearly opposite the register office. We both ordered a gin and tonic and, rather than sipping them slowly, we glugged them down. We did not speak. We were both twitchy. We looked at each other. He went to the bar and got us another two drinks. Those went down fast, too.

'Down the hatch,' he said.

'We'd better go and see if any of them have arrived,' I said, checking my lipstick one more time in a hand mirror.

We went out into the street, blinking. It was rare for us to drink at lunchtime. We giggled and held hands as we crossed the road to the register office. My mother stood in front of the steps leading up to the big oak doors. She looked at my bouquet of white roses and gypsophila. She ignored my husband-to-be as if he was an accessory and searched my face anxiously for any sign of running mascara or blemishes. My stepfather towered above us. He says he has Viking blood. He is often mistaken for a Norwegian and has light blue eyes and blond good looks. My brother and his girlfriend arrived, and then Paul's younger sister, her partner and her son. We wanted a simple, small ceremony and had promised the entire family and our friends a big 'do' when we got to Yorkshire. We were excited about that.

The day went fast. We exchanged vows and rings. We took taxis across Hyde Park to a hotel my mother had booked for a small reception, where we cut a wedding cake she had ordered. Later, we went to a Swedish restaurant, Paul's choice.

We crashed when we got home on our wedding night. We fell asleep immediately. We had to work the next day. There was no honeymoon. We had decided to put our young business first. Holidays, we said, would come later in life. And he had told me earlier in the week, 'I don't feel too good.'

'Do you want to cancel the wedding?'

'No.'

'You'll be fine. The antibiotics will kick in.'

His GP had diagnosed a flu bug.

Acknowledgements

A big thank you belongs to Nicky Ferguson, Lizzie Sherwood and Dr Nicky Stead for your steadfast support, advice, editorial judgement and kindness.

A special thank you goes to Dr Pip Hayes and colleagues at St Leonard's Medical Practice, Exeter, Devon and Royal Devon and Exeter Hospital, and also Jo, Gayle and Emma for your superb care and keeping me upright.

Also, Kerri Sharp and her team at Simon & Schuster, Claudia Martin and Guy Rose, thank you for having faith in me and allowing my voice to be heard. And of course, thank you to my superb legal counsellors in making sure I am not serving time: Paul Worsley QC, Andrew Woolman and John Mewies, our adventure together has made legal history.

I would like to thank my family, especially my mother Betty for her unwavering support, my brother Warwick for bravery, and my stepfather Frank for making me laugh. And a thank you to friends for their continual support, Maja Britton, Jo Clancy and Toker, Mei Chung, Caroline Dennis, Mabroka El Salhi and family, Sarah Fanning, Terri and Peter Frier, Gemma

Green, Darlene Greene, Janet and the Hilltop Riding Stables, Renata Kaczorowska and colleagues, Patrizia Lopez, Donnie and Jan Klatt, Deevah Melendez, Dr Alex Rainer, Migdalia Rivera, Jaime Robles, Dr Tamsyn Rose-Steel and Mike Rose-Steel, all at the Disability Resource Centre (Exeter University), ME/CFS support groups, the Sisters at Noddfa, the Samaritans, Survivors of Bereavement by Suicide and countless other people, too numerous to mention, who have given me constant encouragement and kindness throughout this writing journey. A special thank you goes to the community of Cowick Street, Exeter, especially Faye, Ann and all the Kims. And finally my teachers at the University of Exeter: (ladies first) Professor Helen Taylor, Professor Isobel Armstrong, Professor Karen Edwards, Professor Reginia Garnier, Dr Andy Brown, Professor Philip Hensher, Professor Tim Kendall, Sam North, Professor Steve Neale, Professor Martin Sorrell, Dr Chris Wood. Also the University of Exeter support staff and so many more, again too numerous to mention, as well as my peers, the postgraduate research students, who have advised me to 'never give up'.

Without all of you, I would not have completed this marathon and crossed the finishing line.

ABOUT DIGNITY IN DYING.

WHO WE ARE:
We are a national campaign - a growing movement of people demanding greater choice and control at the end of life. We lobby, inform and educate people on rights at the end of life.

We want everyone to have what they consider to be a good death, including the option of an assisted death for terminally ill, mentally competent adults.

HOW YOU CAN HELP:
We are funded entirely by voluntary contributions from members of the public and without our members we would not be able to continue the vital work we do.

From as little as £20 a year, your membership subscription will enable us to lobby Parliament, advise people on their rights at the end of life, keep Dignity in Dying in the media spotlight and ensure the voices of terminally ill people suffering at the end of their lives are heard.

Your help and support will drive forward our campaign to change the law to allow assistance to die for terminally ill, mentally competent adults.

Join us now and help end unnecessary suffering at the end of life.

....

CONTACT US:

Dignity in Dying
181 Oxford Street
London W1D 2JT

Email: info@dignityindying.org.uk
Telephone: 020 7479 7730

www.dignityindying.org.uk

Dignity
in dying